Training Your Children to Remain in the Vine

Parenting Course: Raising Godly Children

Updated Version

TERITA ST. JULIAN

WESTBOW
PRESS®
A DIVISION OF THOMAS NELSON
& ZONDERVAN

WestBow Press books may be ordered through booksellers or by contacting:

WestBow Press
A Division of Thomas Nelson & Zondervan
1663 Liberty Drive
Bloomington, IN 47403
www.westbowpress.com
844-714-3454

Interior Image Credit: Melanie Taylor of Grace Captured

ISBN: 978-1-9736-2076-1 (sc)
ISBN: 978-1-9736-2075-4 (e)

Library of Congress Control Number: 2018903364

Print information available on the last page.

WestBow Press rev. date: 7/02/2020

CONTENTS

PREFACE

Are you tired of stressing and worrying about your family? Are you concerned about whether you are truly preparing your children to make good choices within such a sinful world? Well, *Training Your Children to Remain in the Vine* is about aligning your whole household to Christ and bringing a powerful godly shift within your thoughts and environment! This entire book is based on one of the most prophetic verses in the Bible, John 15:5. Jesus states, "I am the vine; you are the branches. If you remain in me and I in you, you will bear much fruit; apart from me you can do nothing" (NIV).

If you observe the state of the world and even many Christian households, you will likely notice the perception that people should take full control over their own lives. If that's the case, everyone is in trouble! Wouldn't you rather put your trust and faith in the One who created your mind? God is calling His people to *swiftly* realize that His Word, the Bible, is absolutely true. In order for people to live free from sin, worry, doubt, and everything that is coming their way, parents must be able to raise a generation of children capable of sustaining true Christian principles. God's Word should take precedence over every area of their lives. This book teaches parents the importance of being led by the Spirit of God so they are capable of equipping their children to fight through the many temptations surrounding them. Parents will learn the rewards of living *every day* based on the belief that God *is real* and how to model a life that trains their children to become adults who make godly choices even while living in a world surrounded by sin.

Training Your Children to Remain in the Vine will teach you (the parents) in an accountability format how to free yourselves from carrying the burden of daily stress. This is accomplished by simply learning how to stay attached to Jesus and allow Him to give you the strength to persevere through your difficulties. When you learn the process of thinking like God and acting according to His will, you will be amazed at the things that start to happen supernaturally in your life! This book consists of many stories about the author's journey to get closer to Christ and the amazing ways God transformed her mind.

God is waiting to be much bigger than a weekend church service in your lives. He is waiting for you to truly invite Him into all areas of your life so that He can show out! May your future generations burst forth with godly fruit as God demonstrates His extraordinary plans for their lives. Get ready for your seeds to produce a harvest!

Throughout this book you will learn about:

- the miraculous *power* of the Holy Spirit,

- the joy of staying close to Jesus,

- why your life suffers when you are not connected to Jesus,

- step-by-step ways to get your life in order and make time for God,

- the importance of living by the fruit of the Spirit (referencing Galatians 5:22–23),

- the rewards of fulfilling your purposes in this life, and

- the process of training your children to remain in the Vine.

ACKNOWLEDGMENTS

To my Almighty Father in heaven, Who saved me, Who chose me before I was created to be His vessel, Who covers me with grace, Who supplies me with His underserving mercy, Who prevented me from soaring into the pit of self-destruction and led me to a remarkable life in the Vine, from the depths of my heart, I humbly and gratefully say "Thank You!"

Grandma Lee, Granddaddy, and Uncle Bubba are no longer with us; yet, I thank God for them. Since they believed in Jesus Christ, they, along with my mother, led me to the knowledge of the Lord. I can still remember Grandma Lee humming those old spiritual hymns when life got a little tough to bear. My granddaddy would sit on the porch and read his Bible to me. I remember the story of how Grandma Lee taught him how to read by using that old Bible. I still remember the screeching sound of that paint-chipped rocking chair on the porch, as Uncle Bubba sat in it and sang gospel songs in his deep voice. Year after year, they taught me how to plant seeds, help them grow, and how to patiently expect a harvesting of those seeds. Thankfully those moments are etched into the core of who I am.

Mom, thank you for making me go to church while raising me as a single parent. You still meet more than my needs, show me how to love unconditionally, listen to me, and encourage me along this journey of life! I am *so* blessed to have such a loving mother.

To my Saint, thank you for demonstrating the fruit of the Spirit, sharing this life with me, disciplining our children, and for having faith in God's ability to work through me. I thank God for setting up that divine meeting in 1997!

Avery and Aleesa, thank you for the energy, fun, and Spirit-filled motivational speeches you deliver into my life. I love and appreciate both of you more than words can express!

God has blessed me with great spiritual support from both my family and friends! I really wish that I could name each of you on this acknowledgment page. I actually attempted to do that, but my acknowledgments were turning into another book. Thankfully, you know how much you mean to me. I am so grateful for your prayers, belief in my vision, listening ears, warm hugs, faithful hearts, and, most importantly, *love*!

Thank you to the mother and father of the Rock Family Worship Center, Pastors Rusty and Leisa Nelson, for all the ways that you are a light to this world.

I am also thankful to Pastors Matt and Traci for their prayers and advice, and for the hours they devoted to this book through their editorial suggestions, and their devotion to preparing me for this calling. You are such a blessing to so many families.

Thank you to Pastors Chris and Jamie for leading by example and for being shepherds in our lives.

Thank you, "Olivia (my BFF)" and Kayla Kirkland of Kayla Leanne Photography, Melanie Taylor of Grace Captured Photography, and Andre Terry of Terry Media Group for using your godly talents in such exceptional ways.

And, though she has no idea who I am, thank you to Joyce Meyer for sowing into my life weekly through your television program and books.

May God continue to use many ways to strengthen all of us as He prepares us to fulfill His plans!

Starting Your Journey Agreement

Before proceeding, please know that I have prayed for all of you who will read this book. God knows whom He will select to read it. I have asked Him to give each of you a personal revelation so that you will be aware of what area of your mind, life, and household that He wants to renew, impact, and bless. I believe in the power of prayer, and I hope that either now, or by the time you have completed this book, you will too.

So whether you are husband and wife or single, please read and sign below the statements when you are ready to receive God's guidance in your life; then, take a moment and pray. May God bless you and your family!

I will pray prior to reading the pages of this book and ask God to teach me how to be led by His Holy Spirit, who dwells inside the believers and followers of Christ Jesus. I will continue to pray for my family to be empowered by the Holy Spirit and study the Bible so that I may obtain wisdom and knowledge to understand God's Word and adhere to His directions.

Print (Man of God)   Signature and date

Print (Woman of God)   Signature and date

Why should you and your family have biblical journals?

A journal is your life, your story, and the workings of God through your testimonies. There is no greater gift to leave your family than the spirit of you, created by the Spirit of God. Our memories are our most treasured entities. A combination of events captures the essence of who we are. Your biblical journal is your treasured pathway that builds your faith and may help to place the proper stepping-stones in front of you. It may someday be your most valuable legacy—detailing how you were led to the kingdom and how God blessed your journey. Memories often fade in the faraway places of our minds, but your written prayers and documented events restore the days of long ago. It is your personal story that will lead you to find the ultimate peace in the Lord as you reminisce on the numerous times that God was faithful to you. You will arrive at a place of wonder and be astonished by God's grace and all that He does for you. His love for you will be more visible than ever before leading you to delight in His excellence. Start your journey today by purchasing your journal. Leave your legacy of biblical testimonies, trials, and amazing miracles performed just for you as a gift that may perhaps change generations to come!

CHAPTER 1

The Holy Spirit

The Holy Spirit Is Here!

As a young country girl, I spent most of my weekends either chasing chickens or dodging church folks. I was raised in a little white country church among many Christ-loving people who would hum, groan, rock, and fan themselves during those extended church services. Watching the congregation as they moaned a tune to old gospel hymns became my pastime. As the moans grew deeper and louder, my heart began to race because I thought the Holy Spirit was about to move in! However, He didn't appear to move in me but in what seemed to be almost everyone else!

I was always afraid of the Holy Spirit because when He seemed to show up on the scene, any lady next to me might start flapping her arms around and sock me right in the nose. So I obtained extra "lookout" senses and quick reflexes. I remember thinking, *When the Holy Spirit enters those doors, people will start dancing, shouting, screaming, and running chaotically all over the church!* Sure enough, it always happened like clockwork; when the groans collectively got deeper, people began to holler and wildly scatter. The ushers would frantically run and take off the glasses of some who were filled with the Spirit. Then they would fan others and remove any outer garments such as sweaters or jackets in the attempt to prevent fainting. Yet some fainted anyway.

Unfortunately, back then, we didn't have children's ministry at my church. In addition to that, there wasn't much discussion about the Holy Spirit in my family. So those moments at church were frightening and confusing ones for me. I grew up thinking that the only purpose of the Holy Spirit was to have people act out in strange behaviors. I didn't understand the point of it all.

My own mental confusion prevented me from even publically confessing my life to Christ until I was sixteen, because I kept waiting to have the urge to dance, shout, and scream. Finally, by age sixteen, I felt a little sensation move through my body during service, and I quickly thought, *That must be it!* I hadn't really experienced much of anything all the years prior, so I knew I better act fast before the Spirit left me. I got out of my seat and headed toward the altar to confess that I was *finally* a believer in Christ. As I made my way to the front, I thought, *Is there enough Spirit in me?* So I decided to run instead of walk. I thought, *If I run, I may get more of the Spirit.* So I ran fast! But nope. There wasn't any part of me that wanted to shout, jump around, or scream. My precious grandmother was so happy to see me running to the altar to confess my life to Christ that she ran to meet me. As I stood there, I felt like a liar. I thought at any moment they would know that I couldn't truly have the Spirit and that I wasn't saved.

"Trying" to Act Like a Christian

The next week I tried to act like a Christian and attempted to convince God, myself, and others that I had changed. I decided to help clean around the house and to be extra respectful to my dear mother. I didn't want to talk about this new life because I thought my conversations would reveal that I had not changed due to the fact that nothing felt much different on the inside. I decided to read my King James Bible, but I didn't really understand much of it. So I soon returned to my life of being a "regular" teenager.

With all that running to the altar and cleaning around the house, I thought trying to live up to a Christian lifestyle was too stressful. Yet, over the years, I always believed in God, and I believed that Jesus was the Son of God. I prayed and always felt strongly that there was something more to God and my responsibilities upon this earth than what I was aware of at the time. Yet I still engaged in the typical worldly behaviors, which means it was hard to tell the difference between me and a non-Christian teenager. My life began to reflect the negative music and TV shows that were consuming my mind. My mom thought that she was losing her once sweet, churchgoing daughter to the world—and she was! Mom always insisted that I stay away from drugs, alcohol, and anyone who took part in either of them, so I listened to her for the most part.

Until …

Meeting the "Saint"

At age twenty-one, I met a twenty-nine-year-old man from Louisiana who liked to party, and his name was Saint! Yep, I thought, *If his name is Saint, then he must be one.* He was handsome and a great cook, and we had a ball together—although I knew Mom would not like the fact that drinking alcohol and partying were major parts of his lifestyle. There was never a party without alcohol, and there was almost always a party around him. I didn't know a thing about alcohol, but it didn't take long for me to learn.

After two years of dating, Saint and I married. Though partying and celebrating was part of his culture, he was very loving and thoughtful. I had never seen anyone treat his or her mother with such respect and honor. He gave to people in need and was hardworking. He grew up as a Catholic young man who believed in Christ. Though he had accepted Christ into his heart, his only water baptism was through his Catholic baptismal ceremony at birth. After we were married, he consistently started joining me at my little country church, and being the loving wife that I was, I warned him about my misconceptions regarding the Holy Spirit's entrance. He quickly learned how to protect his nose from the flapping Spirit-filled arms.

Saint later decided to be baptized. We were happy, and we thought life was good! We continued our partying as two worldly Christians.

Until …

God, If That's You, Then Please Send Me a Sign

One day while getting ready for work, out of nowhere I felt a pounding in my chest, and then a powerful sensation that moved through my limbs; tears fell out of my eyes, and there was an overwhelming feeling inside me to get closer to God. I didn't know what had just happened to me. It was the strangest thing that I had ever experienced. I thought I was losing my mind! So I said the prayer that so many of us have said once or twice, "God, if this is really you, then please send me a sign."

Now, first of all, please know that if you are feeling that you need to get closer to God, the One who is going to tell you that is the Holy Spirit. I now understand that what is written in His Word (the Bible) is our sign. Yet, since I was a spiritual novice, God obliged by sending me an alternative sign.

At that time, I had never experienced a feeling like that before. I unknowingly thought that it couldn't be the Holy Spirit because He must only show up at church. (Yep, I had so much to learn.) Later that morning, I entered my workplace with an unsettling feeling inside. I gradually sat down at my desk, looking for a sign from God.

I was searching for anything: a note with the letters G-O-D written on it (in any particular order), a Bible on the printer, or literally a sign that said, "Terita, it's time to get closer to God!" There was nothing like that around me; therefore, I decided that what happened that morning must have been my imagination. So I began to work.

All of a sudden a man who only joked with me weekly walked up and just started talking about God and church. I don't remember him ever saying the word *God* before, yet he picked that day to talk about the Lord! Then he shocked me even more by stating that he was a deacon at his church. I didn't even know he went to church! I was thinking, *What?* I almost fell out of my chair. He proceeded to talk to me about Christ, and everything he said was as if he was holding a big sign over his head saying, "Terita, it's time to get closer to God!"

Shouldn't Thou Start Off Being Like Jesus?

After that day, I decided that it was time for me to change! I prayed to God and asked Him to help me. I was slowly motivated to stop things like drinking alcohol, listening to inappropriate music, and watching a few sinful shows. I was moved at a slow pace to make changes, and I began to read my Bible more. God began to give me clarity and understanding of His Word. Then I started seeing these miraculous things happening in my life.

All of a sudden, I placed extra demands on myself and my husband outside of those that were being gradually led by the Spirit. I wrongfully thought that we had to somehow earn our ability to maintain Christ's acceptance, so I expected my husband and myself to be instantaneously like Christ. Saint hadn't felt the Spirit call him to make the changes that I was trying to implement. My demands on him were causing friction in our marriage. The task seemed too hard, so I started feeling inadequate and imperfect.

So, as you may have guessed, I once again gave up and returned to a life of being a worldly Christian. I returned to watching, listening to, and drinking what I wanted.

It took years, but I later learned that Holy Spirit was dwelling inside me—and that He knew where I was on my spiritual journey the entire time. Christ died to save me from my sins. Since I believed and confessed my sins, He already accepted me for who I was and where I was. God didn't approve of my sins, but He did approve of me. He wanted to bless my life by showing me how to maintain a closer connection with Him by allowing Him to help me turn from sin and begin to live a fruitful life (living a blessed life producing things that please God).

I realized that there was a purpose to my life, and it was to bring joy and blessings, not frustration and sadness. He wanted to show me how to structure my life without feeling anxious or allowing the desire for perfection to hinder my spiritual growth. I learned that all of us are different, and all of us must be led differently by the Spirit. I couldn't tell my husband how to live. I could only pray for him and begin the eventful process of learning to live my life according to the will of God. Saint had to learn how to listen to God, obey, and order his life the way the Spirit was leading him. I learned that though Saint and I are one, our spiritual journeys with the Father have not been the same. Therefore, we cannot control one another or dictate the other's position in relationship with our growth in the Lord. Our roles are to pray for and support one another.

You Mean the Holy Spirit Has a Powerful Purpose?

Through years of experience with the Holy Spirit, I have found Him to be my best friend. I now clearly understand that He didn't just enter those doors of that old church on the weekends, but that He actually lives within the hearts of the believers and followers of Jesus Christ *every day*. All we need to do as believers is to structure our lives by making time for God daily so that the manifestation of the Holy Spirit is revealed, and He can begin to do work in us and through us! He has unique and powerful ways to reshape us internally so that we begin to look less like the world (sin) and more like Jesus.

There is God (the Father in heaven), Jesus (the Son of God in heaven and the Word), and the Holy Spirit (dwells in believers and does the workings of God). Jesus told the disciples before He returned to heaven that He was sending a comforter (the Holy Spirit) to live inside us. His only purpose isn't just to give us goose bumps while listening to a song or cause us to shout or cry. He wants to guide our everyday lives and make changes to us so that we can have prosperous and purposeful lives.

The Bible tells us that the Holy Spirit is our comforter (counselor, helper, advocate, intercessor, strengthener, and standby). He wants to *counsel* us to make the right choices, *help* us whenever we need it, *advocate* or fight for us better than the most expensive attorney, *intercede* to provide blessings for us, *strengthen* us when we feel weak, and just be our *standby* whenever we need Him! If we want to raise godly children, then we most certainly will need all of Him working in and through us!

You may be wondering, *How do I receive all that He has to offer*? Well, it simply starts with you surrendering your heart to the Lord, inviting the Holy Spirit to be a part of your daily life, praying, and studying God's Word. As you spend more time reading the Bible, meditating on His Word, and welcoming the Holy Spirit to consume you, the Spirit will come alive to you in a powerful way. And by doing this, God will work through you to transform your thoughts and actions by the power of His Word. His Word is the truth, and it leads you to live a righteous life. I cannot explain how the Holy Spirit does so much; all, I know is that He has caused my jaw to drop so many times by proving Himself to me in my life and by the testimonies of others as well.

Only the Holy Spirit could have taken me from my worldly mind-set to day-by-day learning how to think a little more like God. When I decided to establish a connection to Christ, He revealed Himself to me through situations. Though it still took me years to desire to have the connection with Him that He always desired to have with me, He was patient as He sought after my heart.

One of our greatest blessings by God is how He supplies us with underserving grace. One of the first things that believers need to really grasp is the fact that we are seen as Christ Jesus to God. When God looks at us, He sees Jesus! Having the ability to represent the name of Christ (Christians) is much bigger than just attending church. Allowing the Holy Spirit to reshape us internally into the image that we already represent to God gives us great power, great responsibilities, and great victories!

Relax—the Holy Spirit Has Designed Your Transformational Plan

The moment in my heart in which I believed and asked for forgiveness, I was saved. I believe I was saved years before I approached the altar at age sixteen, but my misconceptions about the Holy Spirit and religious practices had me confused and searching for something that I had already received. I was waiting for a feeling, but all I needed was belief and faith. "If you declare with your mouth, 'Jesus is Lord,' and believe in your heart that God raised him from the dead, you will be saved. For it is with your heart that you believe and are justified, and it is with your mouth that you profess your faith and are saved" (Romans 10: 9–10 NIV).

I was lacking the knowledge of the Word that I needed to understand salvation, but through the years, the Spirit of God led me to an understanding of His Word, His grace, and His love for me. I was baptized by water at age sixteen after my confession to the church, but it was years later before I was baptized in the fire of God. That baptism is what happened to me when I was getting ready for work that day. Something changed in me! The Holy Spirit was awakening me to the power of God. Though I attempted to return to the world (sinful things), it was hard to enjoy my return because there was an internal battle for my soul, but thankfully, God placed His Spirit inside my heart years ago and declared ownership of His daughter!

John the Baptist stated:

> I baptize you with water for repentance. But after me comes one who
> is more powerful than I, whose sandals I am not worthy to carry.
> He [referencing Jesus] will baptize you with the Holy Spirit and fire.
> (Matthew 3:11 NIV)

Over the years, I got to know more about the Holy Spirit and His power. He prophesied many things that came to fruition in my life. He revealed within my heart things to do, when to wait, or when to turn away. God placed a strong desire inside me to change some things; yet, I still had the ability to make my own decisions. However, it became harder to defy God's wishes because I was beginning to understand how loved I was by Him. I also learned through experiences and trials that if I wanted to have a happy and blessed life, then I had better live by the instructions of God because He is the Creator of life.

As I learned in my youth, the Spirit does cause people to run, flap their arms, shout, cry, faint, and dance! I believe that God's people are headed toward a powerful movement in the church that will lead to spiritual encounters unlike anything that we have ever seen! It may be for us to worship, receive a message from God, transform, heal, etc. Surprisingly, I now find myself worshipping like the people I grew up around in that old church, and I feel so blessed to have the ability to feel the presence of my Father. Yet, unlike I once thought, we don't need those shouting moments to become believers.

Enjoy Your Personal Walk toward Christ

As you begin the process of raising godly children, remember that you are right where you need to be to begin. This is a daily journey, so enjoy it! Getting to know what God is all about and just how much He loves you is fun! You will be amazed to see Him work things out just for you, such as getting you the job you need, blessing you with gifts, transforming your heart to demonstrate His love to complete strangers, teaching you how to hold your tongue, exemplifying the characteristics of Christ to the world, taking away your insecurities, giving you peace during your trials, and delivering your children from the grasp of this world while leading them to their Savior! We cannot raise godly children without the Spirit of God! He speaks to us in many ways: the Word, prayer, thoughts, books, dreams, visions, people, etc.

Please obtain a biblical journal, notebook, or sketchpad (for small children) for each member of your household so that all of you can begin to document prayers, thoughts, Bible verses, teachings, and life experiences as you and your family get closer to Christ. This will be discussed later, but if you have small children, you can journal events for them. It will likely become one of their most prized possessions in life. My journal helps me maintain my faith because it is not just the story of Moses, Abraham, Joseph, or David, but it is my personal story of what God did for me and those within my inner circle. The great thing about my journal is that the stories in it align with the stories in the Bible. This helps to bring an even greater trust and faith in the Word because I am clearly able to see that the faithfulness of God still remains!

Journaling is also a profound way to keep you focused on Christ during those difficult moments. It will bless your lives immensely. As I read through mine, I am astounded by how God changed my life, weaved events together, and led me to this place of peace and unimaginable joy!

Be patient and content with your journey. Saint and I are still working on aligning our lives to the will of God! None of us are exactly the same. We realize that God has a lot more work to do in both of us. He works with us individually as we work together to strengthen one another and our children. Start your journey by journaling your walk with our Father. There's nothing more beautiful and fulfilling than becoming a true Christ follower and watching the Holy Spirit help you answer the call of God upon your life!

Jesus states:

> But I tell you the truth, it is to your advantage that I go away; for if I do not go away, the Helper (Comforter, Advocate, Intercessor–Counselor, Strengthener, Standby) will not come to you; but if I go, I will send Him (the Holy Spirit) to you [to be in close fellowship with you]. (John 16:7 AMP)

Jesus states:

> But when he, the Spirt of truth, comes, he will guide you into all the truth. He will not speak on his own; he will speak only what he hears, and he will tell you what is yet to come. He will glorify me because it is from me that he will receive what he will make known to you. All that belongs to the Father is mine. That is why I said the Spirit will receive from me what he will make known to you. (John 16: 13–15 NIV)

Don't you know that you yourselves are God's temple and that God's Spirit dwells in your midst? If anyone destroys God's temple, God will destroy that person; for God's temple is sacred, and you together are that temple. Do not deceive yourselves. If any of you think you are wise by the standards of this age, you should become "fools" so that you may become wise. For the wisdom of this world is foolishness in God's sight. As it is written: "He catches the wise in their craftiness," and again, "The Lord knows that the thoughts of the wise are futile." So then, no more boasting about human leaders! All things are yours, whether Paul or Apollos or Cephas or the world or life or death or present or the future–all are yours, and you are of Christ, and Christ is of God. (1 Corinthians 3:16–23 NIV)

The Holy Spirit

Summary

- The Holy Spirit dwells inside the hearts of believers.

- When the Spirit of God is upon you, you may sometimes feel a need to react to the overwhelming feelings such as through outbursts, shouts, or wailing.

- The Spirit might also calmly and peacefully place the desire to believe that Jesus is the Son of God in your heart. Thankfully, we are not expected to earn our way into heaven. We just need to believe, ask Jesus to forgive us of our sins, and commit to beginning our journeys closer to Jesus and away from sin.

- The Holy Spirit manifests Himself in our lives by being our powerful comforter (counselor, helper, advocate, intercessor, strengthener, and standby).

- The Holy Spirit wants to guide our individual steps closer to Christ. We cannot be like Jesus in our own strength because we have too many corrupt areas of our lives that must be dealt with through the Spirit of God. Once you consistently study God's Word and learn to seek Him for wisdom, He will guide you toward the areas of your life that may require a transformation.

- Don't get discouraged by trying to rush your or others' relationship with God. The Spirit must lead each of us personally. The best way to lead others to Christ is by showing them your unconditional love and godly lifestyle that can only come from being transformed by Christ.

- An overwhelming amount of joy comes from recognizing God in our daily lives!

- Please obtain a journal for each member of your household. Journaling your walk with Christ helps you later recall all the ways that the Holy Spirit has been your counselor (helper, advocate, intercessor, strengthener, and standby)! Train your children about the goodness of God, and use your and their life experiences to encourage them to make Christ the Lord over all areas of their lives.

CHAPTER 2

The Call

Nothing Godly Happens by Chance

Think about where you spend most of your day. What is that environment like? There are probably some things within your environment that are very tempting or perhaps frustrating, and likely there are many things that are not godly. People, computers, smart phones, music, televisions, or even the view outside your window may have many ways to appeal to your fleshy or earthly temptations. There are so many ungodly things within this world; yet, despite all this, within this moment you were led to learn about aligning your family's life to Christ. No matter where you are in your spiritual walk with Christ, the fact that you could be doing anything else, yet, you are devoting this time to the kingdom of God, speaks volumes about the love God has for you, the power of the Holy Spirit, and your decision to submit your time to the Creator of the world!

God lovingly guides us to Him. If you have been led to give your life to Christ, you know what I mean. You may have felt within the pit of your stomach that the Holy Spirit has called you, saying, "Come to me … Come to me." I wish I could hear about how Christ has been calling you to yield your life to Him. We have no idea about all the times that He sought after us. The fact that you are reading this book is a means by which He is seeking you to answer your call. So whether you are reading it to support me, out of curiosity, someone is practically forcing you, or you are generally concerned about raising godly children, you must be aware that our Father in heaven is not a happenchance God.

The Call

Since you and I are now on this journey together, let me explain how I arrived here. By August 2014, I was thirty-nine years old, and Saint was forty-seven. God had truly blessed us. We had a nice-sized home and prosperous careers. I had a substantial income from a prestigious company and a brand new vehicle that my company purchased for me. My life turned out to be a great accomplishment for a pigtailed little girl who grew up in a single parent household. No one would have guessed that I spent most of my youthful weekends chasing chickens around the yard and dodging church folks. I was very proud of my accomplishments. I was blessed to still have my beautiful loving mother, a handsome successful husband, and, by then, two fantastic kids. We were living the American dream! Due to my success at the company, my husband and I had recently received an all-expense paid trip to Rome, Italy. We *thought* we were having the time of our lives!

Until …

One day, I was upstairs in our home, and I felt this blast of energy surge through my body during prayer. I remembered another powerful time when I felt that feeling during prayer. It was in 2001, when doctors attempted to kindly let me know that my dear grandmother (who ran to meet me at the altar when I was sixteen) would soon die. She had become so ill and weak, and due to her age, they were not able to perform the surgery needed to save her. So the doctor asked me to go home and prepare myself. I was pregnant with my first child and was devastated. I could barely breathe. When I returned home, I dropped to my knees and proceeded to pray and plead to God. During that prayer, I was overcome by forceful bursts of energy, which were followed by a deep thought that was not my own. The words were simply, "Your grandmother will be fine." Along with those words came a sense of peace that engulfed my mind and heart. I returned to the hospital. My grandmother was sent home. She never received the surgery and lived vivaciously for ten more years and into her nineties!

God had been training me to listen to His voice for years. By 2014, I had had many experiences with that feeling, which I now know to be the Holy Spirit. So there I was, having this feeling again. Which left me excited because I knew God was about to tell me something good. I wanted to know the blessings that were coming to my family or a prophetic word concerning something that I needed to know to protect us! However, what I heard in the midst of that powerful feeling was, "I want you to write a book about raising godly children."

Recently, my mind had been bothered by watching some of the actions of the Christian youth become so contradictory to God's Word. Yet, why in the world would God choose unqualified me? Shortly afterward, I heard a preacher say, "God doesn't call the qualified; He qualifies the called!"

My mind was still overwhelmed yet energized by the thought of being called by God. The Spirit of God proceeded to send me an overwhelming sensation to write the outline for the book. The words that were coming in my mind for the outline were moving faster than my hands could write. I wrote down everything that I could. Once the words for the outline stopped flowing, I thought it would be a good time to discuss this with God. I began to question God about this, um, selection.

"God, I am so honored that you have chosen me. Yet, I haven't even accomplished my goal of reading the entire Bible in a year. I am not biblical enough for this. My kids aren't grown yet. With my job and responsibilities, I don't have time to write a book."

You are probably thinking I should have been a lawyer, because I had given God some great objections. So case closed, right?

Well, not exactly. God didn't respond to my counterarguments. And more importantly, He placed this desire in me to see families transformed that was greater than my own desires to be financially successful. I told my husband about it. He had a somewhat hesitant look. However, He had enough experiences with God that he refused to downright object to something that He believed God had requested me to do.

You see years ago, around 2002, Saint and I were in drastic financial distress. Saint worked while I was home taking care of our newborn son. I became convinced that God wanted us to pay our tithes (10 percent of our gross income to the church), so, I talked to Saint about it. He proceeded to look at me as though I was from another planet because we barely had enough money to buy food and diapers. He said that if we had any money left over at the end of the week, then we could give it to the church. Though God had placed a realization inside me that we needed to pay our tithes regardless of how little money we had, God also had placed a realization inside me that I needed to stop arguing with my husband.

So I went to my mother's house and began to pray about the situation with her. Within days, Saint began to break out in blisters on his face; his jaw began to lock up making it difficult for him to eat, and then he lost his job. I prayed harder; then, the Holy Spirit gave me peace and these words were rising in my mind: "Saint will get his job back." So, I began to happily move about the house anticipating a phone call from his previous employer that they wanted him to return to work. In the meantime, Saint thought I was insane. He began to pray asking God to forgive him for whatever he had done and vowed to pay his tithes once he found a job. Within eleven days, God gave him back his job, began to take away his blisters, and restored his ability to eat.

Needless to say, he didn't object to paying our tithes anymore, and he actually had peace about it. We both were amazed to see how though it seemed we didn't have enough to pay our tithes, once we were obedient to God, He blessed us by providing enough money for our tithes and our expenses. I quickly learned that as a wife, it wasn't my place to change my husband or argue with him. All I needed to do was to submit to God and allow Him to do the work that needed to be done in both of us within God's timing.

> Moreover, we have all had human fathers who disciplined us and we respected them for it. How much more should we submit to the Father of spirits and live! They disciplined us for a little while as they thought best; but God disciplines us for our good, in order that we may share in his holiness. No discipline seems pleasant at the time, but painful. Later on, however, it produces a harvest of righteousness and peace for those who have been trained by it. (Hebrews 12:9–11 NIV)

Since, I have kept journals since 2002, they helped us recall many past experiences that showed how our obedience to God became a blessing, so God gave Saint peace about the book. Once I had Saint's approval, I began to write. However, I barely talked with Saint or the kids because I was devoting so much of myself to it, and I didn't know how I would be able to complete the task. Well, God always has a plan, but we may not always like or understand the beginning stages of His plan.

What Do You Do When Your Obedience Starts Off Feeling Like a Curse?

The next week after starting on the book, I was in an elevator reporting to work when I felt these words whispering to my heart, "This is the last day you will do this job." Immediately, I was flooded with a feeling of sadness and a reality that the thought may be true. I visited a business acquaintance and said, "This may be my last day on the job." Now our company had a merger, so I knew that things were shifting; however, I didn't think that shift would involve me. I was recently one of the top representatives in the entire company. Nevertheless, the next day, I received a phone call from HR in which the representative stated that my position was displaced (meaning the day prior was my last day on the job!). My mind immediately returned to the previous day in the elevator. I learned that the Holy Spirit doesn't just speak to me in a powerful way; sometimes He just whispers. My heart was in shambles. I felt embarrassed, confused, and alone. How was I going to tell my family?

Well, they were supportive. My husband and I still agreed that I would write the book, and then quickly rush back to work so I could make some money. However, it took a *little* longer than we expected.

The next year was an eventful one. You see, God needed to clear me from the world so that He could cleanse me of a large portion of mental corruption that I obtained throughout the years within this world. I had developed a soul that was kind, generous, and loving, yet intertwined with a portion of pride, competitiveness, self-centeredness, and revengefulness. Yet, for some reason, God still selected me even before I was created to complete this calling. I realized that He had been preparing me for years by using the Holy Spirit, my experiences, my unusual mental thinking abilities, and His Word to put the book together. I spent the next year studying His Word, attending church services, praying, worshiping, speaking with pastors, reading spiritual books, listening to biblical teachings, interviewing parents, volunteering to teach Bible study to inner-city children, training my own children, cleaning the house, cooking, scrubbing the toilets, spending time with Hubby, catching up with family/friends, making new friends, encouraging those around me, volunteering where needed, and writing the book. Whew … Finally, I finished the book! *Yippee,* right?

Uh-Uh …

What do you do when being obedient to God feels more like a curse than a blessing? You keep being obedient to God!

Nothing Is Finished… Until God Says, "It's Finished!"

I had to start over! God was leading me to explain how a parent's willingness to be led by the Holy Spirit is the key to raising godly children. I believe He wanted me to show many of our family's shortcomings and His unfailing love and grace through it all. He was also leading me to design the book so that it could be used as a teaching tool. I kept thinking, *I was finished with the book, and now I'm starting over? People are going to think that I'm crazy! We are running out of money! My husband is going to leave me for a sane woman! How is my mom still supporting me through all this? Is she okay?*

I felt like turning my back on this calling!

Until …

I talked to my kids about it, and my four-year-old daughter said, "Mom, God doesn't make mistakes!" And my twelve-year-old son said, "God is with you!" Not only was God working on me, but He was working on my family. So here we are. I chose to trust and believe in God. I prayed for strength; I read Hebrews chapter 11, and then I read powerful moments of my biblical journal. I said to myself, *We are not going to run out of money! Our story is going to bless people! God has a plan! I am thankful that He chose me to carry it through, and nothing is finished until God says it is finished!*

So you are now reading book two, in which book one will probably never reach the world, but I found that God was with me the entire time, and He didn't make a mistake. Every step of this journey was part of the plan. As my loving mother recently reminded me, our success in life isn't based on the temporal but the eternal. My career plans are the temporal, but God has now called me to help build the kingdom of God—that is the eternal!

We must live and be able to function in this temporal world, but believers in Christ are also called to be focused upon things that are eternal. All of us have a specific assignment to bring others closer to Jesus. In addition to that, if you are a parent, raising godly children is one of the most important "calls" upon your life. I am so excited that you have made the decision to answer "The Call!" Please share your experiences to help others as you transition toward this life of training your children to remain in the Vine!

CHAPTER 2
The Call

Summary

- There are so many things that are attempting to pull you deeper into the world and farther from Christ.

- The Spirit of God intercedes by arranging things in your life and gives you godly wisdom.

- Be joyous about the fact that *you* have a godly purpose in this life.

- When you feel that the Holy Spirit is leading you to do something, pray about it, and ask for the right opportunity to move forward. You will find that God has already made plans to lead you through the journey. It may seem like a bumpy journey, but each bump can allow you to be better prepared for the next one.

- Answering the call of God means that not every moment will likely be easy, but thank God for those difficult moments because they will help develop your faith and often lead to incredible testimonies as you walk through them.

- Take comfort in knowing that God loves you, will never leave you, and that His plan is without error.

- Get ready to answer the call of training your children to remain in the Vine and lead them toward the gift of eternal life!

CHAPTER 3

"I Am the Vine; You Are the Branches"

Jesus states,

I AM THE VINE; YOU ARE THE BRANCHES. IF YOU REMAIN IN ME AND I IN YOU, YOU WILL BEAR MUCH FRUIT; APART FROM ME YOU CAN DO NOTHING. (JOHN 15:5 NIV)

Carnation Confirmation

Sometimes, we may have read a verse such as John 15:5 in the Bible our entire lives, before it finally hits us. One day, I gave my four-year-old daughter a single carnation, in which she was just thrilled. She danced and played with it so much that I didn't know how it was still hanging on.

Then, she said, "I can't wait to sleep with it tonight!"

I looked around. "Huh? Sweetie, you can't sleep with a flower because you will knock all the pedals off."

She asked, "Well, where are we going to put it tonight?"

I said, "We will put it in a vase of water so it will live longer."

She sadly stated, "What do you mean live longer?"

I began to explain vines and how things live and grow. I told her that the flower had to remain attached to the vine to live but that by putting it in water, we'll maintain its life for a couple days.

She looked at me sadly and stated, "If I were a flower, I would always remain in the vine."

All she could see was that the flower had so much beauty and potential; but it was all wasted because once it was no longer on the vine, it would soon wither and die.

Well, the only thing I learned that day was to never give this child another flower. But when I was seeking God for the name of this book, He truly awakened me to the fact that there was a purpose to that day with my daughter, and I was certainly not on this book journey alone. I had been trying to come up with my own title. Finally, I decided to ask God. After all, this book was His idea. I figured that a major decision like choosing the title should come down the chain to little ole me anyway. I prayed and waited patiently in silence. While waiting, I felt a thundering inside my chest, and the words in my spirit said, *Training Your Children to Remain in the Vine!* When the title surfaced within my mind, then came the image of that day with my daughter and the carnation. During that prayer I could also remember her stating, "If I were a flower, I would always remain in the vine."

Then, God led me to this scripture in the Bible:

Jesus states:

> I am the vine; you are the branches. If you remain in me and I in you, you will bear much fruit; apart from me you can do nothing. (John 15:5 NIV)

Later, I turned on the TV to watch my favorite TV evangelist, Joyce Meyer. Guess what! She had a flower on the stage next to her, and she began teaching about John 15!

It was just another sign that the Holy Spirit was guiding me through this process! I was so excited and energized because not only did God give me the title; He confirmed it and reaffirmed it! He's so good!

Branches Need "The Vine"!

So if Jesus is the Vine, and we are the branches, what is the significance of this relationship? Since I was certainly not a botanist, I needed more knowledge about the relationship between vines and branches other than the little information I gave to my four-year-old. After my research, this is what I concluded:

Branches need vines to live! Oh yeah, we already knew that, huh?

The only way we can live is through Christ. If Jesus is the Vine, then He is letting us know that we as branches cannot live without Him. When Jesus left heaven and came to provide us with eternal life, like us, He was faced with temptations. Yet, He overcame every one of those temptations so that you and I would be saved! And His overcoming power of the Holy Spirit desires to give us the ability to overcome sin too.

Jesus shed His blood for our sins. He represented our sin and became the perfect sacrifice by dying upon the cross. Can you envision the thoughts within His mind or the depth of His prayers to God prior to His crucifixion? The Bible gives us some insight into this.

Jesus states:

> "Father, if you are willing, take this cup from me; yet not my will, but yours be done." An angel from heaven appeared to him and strengthened him. And being in anguish, he prayed more earnestly, and His sweat was like drops of blood falling to the ground. (Luke 22:42–44 NIV)

That verse really helped me understand that Jesus knows what stress, temptation, turmoil, despair, and internal conflict feels like better than any of us; yet, He persevered and did the will of His Father! Since Jesus needed strengthening from the angels, this should allow each of us to realize that Jesus understands the struggles within us. Therefore, He left us with the Holy Spirit so that we too can fulfill God's plans for our lives.

As a child, I always visualized Jesus just gracefully dying on the cross. I didn't understand the battle that must have been raging within Him or the suffering that He endured while leading up to His death. I now realize that not only did He save us of our sins by dying on the cross, He taught us how to handle temptations. Essentially, He gave us the way to live eternally, but He showed us how to live in a temporal world by focusing on the eternal and fighting our battles in prayer.

Jesus represents the Vine, or the eternal life, and if we want to stay attached to the Vine, we as branches must be like the Vine. Our lives must be like the life of Christ. If you are saying, "My behavior is so far away from being like Christ," don't worry, because so are the majority of us in the world. The Bible tells us that we are born sinners. It is important to understand that before we can train our children to remain in the Vine, we must learn how to strengthen our little branches so that we can demonstrate to our children the ways to stay connected to Christ and live fruitful lives. We must learn how to pray even when we feel defeated and distant from Christ. Like the angels strengthened Jesus, God will also strengthen us to handle whatever difficulties that we face.

Transformation of Our Soul: Think, Feel (Emotions), and Will

We all have souls that are a combination of what we think, how we feel (emotions), and our will. Our soul is often corrupted by many things of the world. It gets corrupted by our environment through what we view, our communications, what we listen to, our upbringing, the way we have been treated, and sometimes just the lifestyles that we have chosen. When we become saved, we should desire to please the Lord by being willing to receive the wisdom that the Holy Spirit is sending us and start allowing God to help us filter out of our lives things that contradict His Word. Please understand that Jesus is not bewildered by the corruptness of our souls. He just wants us to be willing to make changes to our lives so that the Holy Spirit can guide us toward aligning our souls to God's will. When we begin the process of thinking like God, we are able to help save our children and others.

We are all different! I have heard of some people who are saved and seem to have a renewing of their mind instantly. You may have seen them cursing and drunk on Monday, but after Tuesday's transformation, they are preaching by Sunday. Not really, but you get the idea. Yet others may be like me; so, God may have to exclude them from things to renew their minds. Then there's some like Saint, who will learn to make small changes over the years in which one day they may look at their lives and realize that God had shifted many things around for the better. Once you are a willing branch and have decided that you will remain in the Vine, you will be surprised to see how over time God will start to restructure things. Yet, it all starts with your choice to sometimes yield your life to God and give up some things. As we say in our home, then, God will "show out" in a powerful way!

Once your soul begins to align with the way God thinks (the Word), how He would feel and His will, you are establishing a firmer connection in the Vine. God has very creative ways for aligning our souls to His will. Let me give you an example.

God had already led my family to become givers. We had begun to set aside a substantial portion of our monthly expenses to pay our tithes, offerings, charities, and to help others around us in need. Don't think I am bragging because we wouldn't have done any of that without the Spirit of God. In addition to that, God often blessed us when we were obedient to His Word. Yet, He somehow trained us to love to give because we love, not to love to give because we love to get! He is just so awesome!

We were recently big givers with the funds to give, but our faith was strengthened when the funds were no longer as accessible yet God still expected us to give. After God separated me from my employer to focus on the book, He continued to provide for us. Yet, when I was led to rewrite the book, money had started dwindling way down. I believe we still needed to establish more faith and an ability to trust Him like that bird in Iowa does for his worms each week.

Oh yeah, He cares for and knows each bird individually. So when you are feeling discouraged or having a lack of faith, pick a state and imagine a bird there. Then visualize God leading that bird to worms. (Hey, how often do you see worms just crawling around? It's not that easy!) Yet, all these birds are still living. Just like me writing this book or you reading it; that's not happenchance. The Bible tells us that we are worth more than the fowls of the air. We need to have confidence in that fact!

Jesus states,

> Look at the birds of the air; they do not sow or reap or store away in barns, and yet your heavenly Father feeds them. Are you not much more valuable than they? Can any one of you by worrying add a single hour to your life? (Matthew 6:26–27 NIV)

Yep, Jesus sure *told* us!

Anyway, though our money was scarce, we continued to pay our tithes, offerings, and charities; yet, our extra giving amount was reduced, which made one day a special bird-like faith building moment. I was encouraging a friend to have faith in God because her bank account was overdrafted. I barely had enough money for my groceries; otherwise, I would have been more than happy to help her. After our conversation, I hugged her and walked away. I had made up my mind that I would pray for her. As I walked away, I could feel the Lord calling upon me to give her a portion of what I had. You can visualize me shaking my head like a dog trying to clear that thought from my mind. I'm thinking, *Now, God, you know I gave when I had it to give. We even pay above our tithes. But, if I give her this, then I won't have enough money for my groceries.* The next thought in my mind was, *Okay, was it you who was just teaching her about having faith?*

Yep, He sure *told* me!

I didn't know how much she needed; I just walked back to her and gave her the amount I felt the Lord was asking me to give. Afterward, I reluctantly proceeded to the grocery store with a minimal amount of faith that I would have enough cash for my groceries. I didn't calculate the items in my buggy. There was just a little part of me trying to believe that God was watching out for me. Upon stacking all my groceries on the counter, it looked as though I had gone way over the amount I had available.

But, the power of God …

When the register totaled my transaction, it was the *exact* amount that I had in cash! I was praising God in my head, and fighting tears, as I pushed my cart to the car! When I returned to the car, trying to gather my emotions, I received a text from my friend. It stated, "The amount that you gave me was the *exact* amount I needed to pay my overdraft!" So much for fighting back the tears. I began to praise the Lord while sitting in my car. At any moment, you would have thought that an usher would have shown up in that grocery store parking lot to remove my glasses and sweater! (Hee-hee, thank God for ushers.) Seriously, though, that was definitely a biblical journal moment!

God was teaching us to trust Him in "all" things. He began to align our souls to His will by training us that our decisions should never be based on our perceived circumstances but on the direction that was given to us by the Holy Spirit. Later, I cooked our meal and noticed we had an excess amount of food. Now, all my life, I am embarrassed to say that I threw food away if we had too much. Yet, this time was different. This is another example of how the Holy Spirit began to slowly make a positive change in our lives. In this humbling moment, it felt as though I needed to repent if I threw that food in the trash. So I contacted Mrs. Fran, who is the head of Manna House, which is a place dedicated to feeding and providing for those in need. She told me that she would give it to a family in need. All of a sudden my mind was renewed in the area of giving, and

I couldn't believe all the times I had wasted an opportunity to bless someone with a simple home-cooked meal. Though we were giving when we had plenty; we became even more like Christ when we became givers when we had little. God had just transformed a new area of our souls.

I'm sure you get it now; we want our souls to be like Jesus. We should want to learn how to think and love like God! Living like Jesus is fun! Not only will your lives be blessed, but you will have an inner confidence that God is on your side! No matter what you go through or must face, you can act like Jesus did before the crucifixion. Pray to our heavenly Father, and He will strengthen you, and the Spirit of God will direct you. Over time, you can become full believers that good things are ahead of every struggle because even death leads to life for a believer! One of the best things you can teach your children about remaining in the Vine is to teach them to remain faithful even during trials. Life will provide the difficult experiences, but the way you handle those difficulties in front of your children will provide a large part of the training needed to prepare them for their own life in the Vine!

CHAPTER 3

"I Am the Vine; You Are the Branches"

Summary

Jesus states:

> I AM THE VINE; YOU ARE THE BRANCHES. IF YOU
> REMAIN IN ME AND I IN YOU, YOU WILL BEAR MUCH
> FRUIT; APART FROM ME YOU CAN DO NOTHING.
> (JOHN 15:5 NIV)

- Branches need to remain attached to the vine to live. Since Jesus used the analogy in John 15:5 that He is the Vine, and we are the branches, then, He is telling us that we must remain attached to Him to live.

- Jesus demonstrated how to live by focusing on the eternal not the temporal.

- If we want to be attached to the Vine, then we must learn how to become like the Vine.

- Our soul is comprised of how we think, how we feel (emotions), and our will.

- The sinful things within our environment and what we choose to allow into our sight, ears, and minds can corrupt our souls.

- We must allow the Holy Spirit to renew our minds by being willing to filter things out of our lives that are attempting to suppress our ability to align our souls to God's will.

- We must allow the Holy Spirit to build our faith through experiences and learn to walk in faith as Jesus did on earth.

- We cannot base our faith on our perceived circumstances but on the Word, which is the truth.

CHAPTER 4

"If You Remain in Me and I in You"

Part 1: Manifestation of the Supernatural Power Of God

Jesus states:

> I AM THE VINE; YOU ARE THE BRANCHES. IF YOU REMAIN IN ME AND I IN YOU, YOU WILL BEAR MUCH FRUIT; APART FROM ME YOU CAN DO NOTHING. (JOHN 15:5 NIV)

Grieving the Holy Spirit

Ask yourself if you are committed to living a life in the Vine of Jesus. If you are still reading, the answer is likely yes! That is wonderful! I hope you have signed the "Starting Your Journey Agreement" at the beginning of the book. You will be blessed by the commitment that you are making to Christ. When I got to the "If you remain in me and I in you" part of the verse, I thought, *How am I going to train people to remain in Jesus?* As you know, my branch was dangling many times. I often heard pastors preaching about how they accepted Christ and never returned to the things of the world. I thought there must be something wrong with me because I sadly turned from our Lord. However, I now understand that I was normal. Though I never stopped believing in Christ, I didn't truly believe that all the words/phrases in the Bible by faith could manifest themselves supernaturally in my life. Friend, let me just state, "If you feel this way, you couldn't be more deceived!"

Once I began to journal and started looking back over my situations and circumstances, I realized that many of my experiences correlated with what the Bible stated, and I began to see God in a new light. I learned how to appreciate my journey closer to God and realized that God works all things for the good of those who love Him and who have been called according to His purpose (referencing Romans 8:28). The important part of my journey is that I someday reach my destination (Heaven) and hopefully pick up many others along the way. Sometimes our wrong turns enable us to clearly direct others back to the main road. If I had never taken a wrong exit, perhaps I might not be able to guide someone else.

After God pulled me away from my career for a time to focus on the book, He revealed to me how I had reverted back to the world throughout some of the years of my life. It wasn't just my desire for perfection that caused me to get off track. Over time, I started watching movies that made me less sensitive to certain types of sin. I listened to some secular music that in turn filled my mind with whatever corrupt thought was being created by the words within the songs. There were business parties filled with worldly conversations in which I began to take part. Once my career path started rising, I focused more on my selfish ambitions. I became highly competitive, judgmental, and cunning. When I encountered people who were ruthless, instead of praying for them, I developed strategies to reveal their deceitfulness.

Please understand that God calls His people into many different professions; however, we have to prayerfully not allow those professions to transform us into something different than what God called us to be. I had subconsciously allowed my soul to be corrupted by the world instead of being the light in the career where God had placed me. I prayerfully believe that I will return to my profession someday, but this time, I will let God's light shine through me, and by the power of the Holy Spirit, the whole environment will change!

Due to my previous bad choices, it became difficult for me to recognize the Spirit of God in my daily activities and to receive the power of the Spirit of God in my life. The sinful things that may appear small to many are the very things that may actually grieve (sadden) or quench the Holy Spirit. And do not grieve the Holy Spirit of God [but seek to please Him], by whom you were sealed [branded as God's own] for the day of redemption [the final deliverance from the consequences of sin] (Ephesians 4:30 AMP).

Since, I was grieving the Holy Spirit, I didn't feel Him as my comforter (counselor, helper, advocate, intercessor, strengthener, and standby). This suppressing of the power within me led me to often feel like a Christian trying to rely upon my own strength. So many Christians are trapped in this place right now. It leads to frustration, worrying, doubting, confusion, and sometimes just utter chaos in our lives. It can also cause us to be prideful because we give ourselves credit for our achievements.

During my time of grieving the Holy Spirit, I still went to church, read my Bible, and gave. I do not want any of you to continue on the path of deception that I was on for so long. That's why I want to make sure you understand that the negative things that you choose to listen to, view, and surround yourselves with can likely have an impact on your spiritual development. Be wise and selective in your choices because you are created for a higher purpose, and no one can give you the type of joy that comes from God! God wants to transform your life and bless you in ways you can't imagine! After you have received direction from God, begin to yield to Him in obedience. It's not always easy at first; but, afterward, you will likely be astonished by His profound presence in your life!

Yielding to God doesn't mean that all your problems will vanish. I can almost guarantee that they won't, and this may sound weird, but you need to be thankful that they won't.

Out of some of my toughest times came a powerful revelation about God's love for me. When we persevere through our trials the way God directs us, the Spirit of God can help us mature in Christ and can give us an awareness of how far we have come. "Consider it pure joy, my brothers and sisters, whenever you face trials of many kinds, because you know that the testing of your faith produces perseverance. Let perseverance finish its work so that you may be mature and complete, not lacking anything. (James 1:2–4 NIV)

The Holy Spirit can bring peace and joy even during a trial; and, at times, your obedience, faith, and God's love may lead to a supernatural intervention in your circumstance. Through the supernatural realm, the Spirit of God can work something out on your behalf that would be almost impossible for it to just be a coincidence. Those moments are spectacular and definitely journal worthy, especially when the Holy Spirit intercedes during a trial!

The Power of Obedience

Another day in 2002, I was at home saying my prayers when all of a sudden I could feel a pounding within my heart and these words started rising, "Stop watching *one of my favorite* soap operas." I won't give the name of that soap opera, but you can just fill in the blank with any one of them that appeals to you. I know most people don't admit to watching soap operas anymore, but I know many of you are because they are still on TV.

Anyway, I have to allow you to understand the significance of this request from God. I l-o-v-e-d this particular soap opera! I had been watching it with my grandmother since I was three years old. (Hey, don't judge my precious grandma! Hee-hee) In 2002, my grandmother was still alive, and this was still our show! The characters were like family to us. They weren't just actors. I can still remember playing outside as a child, and hearing my grandma yell, "Our show is on!" I would even stop chasing a chicken to watch this show. I remember all the laughs we had over the years about the actors, and all the times we thought someone on the show was dead, but then they would reappear. I recalled the number of marriages that the main character had on the show. This had become part of my life and my bonding time with my loving grandma. And now, God was telling me to give it up! I was hoping that this couldn't be God!

However, I gave it up.

Then, I went into a slight depression mode. I felt like I was missing the most important part of my day. Sad huh? I was led to replace that time with praying, listening to worship music, or reading my Bible. I was also led to start my biblical journal then as well. This is the very first journal entry I made: "November 18, 2002. Feeling down. (Referencing God's commands here) Told not to watch (soap opera). Hard to imagine. I look forward to it so much. Afraid of not holding on to spiritual lifestyle. But I remember how bad I feel when I don't. I pray that You (God) will help me when it is time for teaching in January and let your words come through."

Wasn't that soap opera addiction pitiful? I mean, seriously—I didn't think that I could maintain an amazingly powerful life with God because of a man-made TV show? Hopefully, one day you will be able to laugh about some things that were holding you back too. I hope I get to hear about some of them and laugh with you! Now, I don't know what that teaching comment was referencing back then, but I don't think it is a coincidence that my very first journal entry is about being obedient to the Holy Spirit, the consequences that I face if I don't, and allowing His Words to enable me to teach. Wow, God!

Now, let me tell you what happened after I was obedient and released this soap opera from my life.

As you likely recall, during that time of our lives, we didn't have much money. Saint and I had just been married for a few years, and our son was a baby. We had just gone through that difficult situation that led Saint to submit to God by paying his tithes. All of our needs were being met, but I still desired to have a little extra money each month. I tried to have our house refinanced, but every refinance company that I called said they couldn't do it. I was so sad. I thought, *God, we are paying our tithes. I am not watching "The Show." I am spending more time with You. Why aren't You helping us more with our finances?* I didn't receive an answer, but I did receive a spiritual knowledge to just trust Him.

I decided to just forget about the refinancing. Days later, I was paying our bills online through a computerized banking service. It was different than the online banking systems we use through our standard banks today. I had all my bills listed there that I needed to pay. I entered the dollar amount of all the bills and tried to click *submit* for each individual biller. However, when I attempted to pay our mortgage, the computer gave me an error message. It allowed me to pay all the other bills except the mortgage. I was so frustrated because the bill was due in a few days, and I didn't have time to mail a check. I didn't want to pay it by phone because we would have to pay an extra fee, and at this point every dollar mattered. Yet, I had no other choice.

In frustration, I called the mortgage company to pay the bill by phone. Oh great, I happened to get the chipper representative who liked to talk. "Okay, I can process this payment for you right away Mrs. St. Julian. Let me just get my computer program up. So … where do you live?"

By this point, I was not in the mood for small talk. Yet, the time with God had trained me to be kind; though, I wasn't feeling kind because I couldn't even watch my show. "Alabama," I stated. Then out of courtesy not curiosity, I asked, "Where do you live?"

"Texas," he said. "Have you ever been to Texas?" he asked.

I responded while hoping his computer program would speed it up, "Yes, we have family there."

He was so excited and then had the nerve to ask, "What are their last names?"

I'm thinking, *What?* This guy is really nosy, and he needs a computer upgrade like me! I tried to sound like that wasn't an inappropriate question by kindly stating, "They are Moutons."

He said, "I had a girlfriend that was a Mouton." He tells me her first name and exactly where she grew up.

At that point, I was in complete shock because due to the name and the area he described, I knew that was our cousin! I thought, "Should I tell him, or should I just let it go because if he knows, then this conversation may never end?" I realized that I had to tell him because that coincidence was just too good to keep to myself. So, I cheerfully stated, "That's my cousin!"

Needless to say, he was so excited, and we laughed and talked about how ironic it was for two random people to find out they were connected in some way to the same individual from the second largest state in the United States all while talking on the phone for a couple of minutes. I was rather entertained by that but summed it up as a coincidence.

Until …

After he processed the bill payment, we hung up the phone. He called me back that same day and said, "Hi, I wasn't supposed to say anything, but you feel like family now. We can actually refinance your mortgage for you at no additional cost and reduce your payments by several hundred dollars a month. Would you be interested?"

God is so good! "Yes!"

That refinance went through flawlessly, and it ended up saving us more money than all the mortgage companies that I had previously contacted would have been able to offer. That is the supernatural power of God!

We have had so many moments like that one that made it as biblical journal entries. God taught me how to remain in the Vine by detaching myself from a very powerful thing that was holding my mind captive to the world, "The Show." Once I was willing to make the decision to remain in the Vine and to be obedient to God's instructions about how to establish my life there, God was ready to grow me in faith and move me away from being a Christian unaware of the plans that God had for my life. The Holy Spirit began to manifest Himself in my life as my comforter (counselor, helper, advocate, intercessor, strengthener, and standby). Think about how the Holy Spirit functioned in each of those roles during that refinancing situation. I want you to experience that power in your lives as well!

I learned how to remain in the Vine, and Jesus remained in me. He wouldn't allow me to be rude to the representative on the phone. Though I was frustrated, if I had given in to my fleshly emotions, I would have missed my blessing during what was feeling like an inconvenience at the time. Since then, I have had many situations where God has strengthened my ability to be content on the inside and outside. In that situation, I was being kind because I felt that it was the right thing to do, but now God has strengthened me to sincerely be kind during times of frustration without having to put forth such an effort.

When your children see Christ show through you on those nonchurchy feeling days, they too will learn how to exemplify Christ to the world. Remember that you need the Holy Spirit active in you to obtain the ability to receive all of what God has for you!

CHAPTER 4

"If You Remain in Me and I in You"

Part 1: Manifestation of the Supernatural Power Of God
Summary

Jesus states:

> I AM THE VINE; YOU ARE THE BRANCHES. IF YOU
> REMAIN IN ME AND I IN YOU, YOU WILL BEAR MUCH
> FRUIT; APART FROM ME YOU CAN DO NOTHING.
> (JOHN 15:5 NIV)

- Grieving the Holy Spirit prevents us from experiencing some of the benefits and power that God wants to demonstrate in our lives.

- The Holy Spirit doesn't leave believers; however, we need to remain in Him so that He will be present to us in our lives.

- Without the manifestation of the Spirit of God, we become weak because we begin to depend upon ourselves for strength.

- Obey God when He leads you to stop doing something or to start doing something because He has an awesome plan just for you. Don't abandon God's plans if things get difficult because you may be approaching one of the most remarkable testimonies of your life!

- God doesn't want us to sit back and not work; however, when difficult times arise, He wants us to take comfort in knowing that He will make a way for us. Pray and plan your ways, then let Him guide your steps. There is nothing more exciting than watching things that seem impossible become supernaturally possible because of the love of Christ.

CHAPTER 4

"If You Remain in Me and I in You"

Part 2: The War

Jesus states:

> I AM THE VINE; YOU ARE THE BRANCHES. IF YOU
> REMAIN IN ME AND I IN YOU, YOU WILL BEAR MUCH
> FRUIT; APART FROM ME YOU CAN DO NOTHING.
> (JOHN 15:5 NIV)

Satan Is Real

Remaining in the Vine may be easy for some, but in the past it wasn't for me because I was a Christian trying to hold on to the sinful things I enjoyed in this world. God showed me how those attachments can cause us to detach ourselves from Christ! I know that I'm not the only Christian who has lost my focus upon Christ; yet, many people rarely discuss this with one another. While working on book two, God revealed three words to me: time, awareness, and discipleship.

Oh yeah, you can imagine that I needed a little more information than that to deliver a message to all of you. Okay, a lot more information! It felt as if the Spirit of God said to me, "The more time we devote to God, the more aware we become of God, Satan, and discipleship. On the contrary, the more time we devote to the world, the less aware we become of God, Satan, and discipleship." Part 3 of this chapter will explain this in detail, but for now let's discuss why we need to be aware of Satan.

Now, you haven't heard me mention Satan. However, the underlying issues in our lives derived from Satan and our unwillingness to combat him at a given time. Satan is real. He is not a man with horns dressed in a red costume holding a pitchfork. God actually created him to be one of His angels in heaven. Yet, Satan's pride overcame him, and he wanted to be worshipped like God. He actually convinced some angels in heaven to help him wage a war against God. Now, I have met some persuasive people in my time, but none quite like that. Due to ignorance, it may have been intriguing for angels to listen to some of his plans, but if he started talking about waging a war against God, I think that's when I would have flapped my angel wings and flown around Heaven far away from him.

Seriously, I hope by now you are aware of how even allowing your minds to get entertained by evil is an attempt to mentally trap your soul.

> Then war broke out in heaven. Michael and his angels fought against the dragon, and the dragon and his angels fought back. But he was not strong enough, and they lost their place in heaven. The great dragon was hurled down–that ancient serpent called the devil, or Satan, who leads the whole world astray. He was hurled to the earth, and his angels with him. (Revelation 12:7–9 NIV)

That scripture makes me want to say, "Really, God? Satan was sent down here with us?" Read that scripture carefully because it wasn't just Satan sent here but also the angels he tricked. And by looking at the state of earth, it must be a whole heap of them! However, as my children once told me, "God doesn't make mistakes, and He is with us!"

> For our struggle is not against flesh and blood, but against the rulers, against the authorities, against the powers of this dark world and against the spiritual forces of evil in the heavenly realms. Therefore, put on the full armor of God, so that when the day of evil comes, you may be able to stand your ground, and after you have done everything, to stand. Stand firm then, with the belt of truth buckled around your waist, with the breastplate of righteousness in place, and with your feet fitted with the readiness that comes from the gospel of peace. In addition to all this, take up the shield of faith, with which you can extinguish all the flaming arrows of the evil one. Take the helmet of salvation and the sword of the Spirit, which is the word of God. (Ephesians 6:12–17 NIV)

That verse tells us that we had better be armed for a war! I feel as though we need to get a sketchpad and draw all the items we need, or check them off a list. If something is missing, find it! However, all believers really need is to have faith and listen to the Holy Spirit (which speaks to us through: the Word, prayer, thoughts, books, dreams, visions, people, etc.) and be willing to obey.

We all like to think that if we were angels in heaven, we would have recognized Satan's tricks the moment he planned on waging a war on God; however, I am not so sure. While on earth, God has given us His Word, ability to pray/worship anytime, and the Holy Spirit to live inside believers to give us guidance and comfort. Yet, we don't always put on the full armor of God, leaving many to be tricked by Satan. He doesn't just walk up to us and say things like, "Misty, I want you to watch an inappropriate show in front of your children, so they will grow up imitating those sinful behaviors." Oh, pleeeaaassse, he is way smarter than that! He has a girlfriend call you during the moment your child walks in the room, and says, "Girl, put the TV on channel 000, there is a man on there that you have to see right now!" He wants to occupy our minds with things of the world, or entice us to find entertainment in the very things that placed Jesus on the cross in an attempt to entangle himself around our branches until they finally snap.

Our War Is Not Man against Man but Satan against God

You see, Satan has one main mission and that is to ultimately kill, steal, and destroy by ensuring that we go to Hell along with him. He has nothing to lose. He is not powerful enough to destroy God, but he is powerful enough to destroy God's children if he can detach them from the Vine of Jesus or keep them unattached. It is very simple; Satan uses every strategy possible to align our souls to his will. Probably one of the most strategic tactics he uses on Christians is to send people to mistreat us. You might have been at church all weekend, but then on Monday morning someone who always irritated you makes the most outlandish comment that just sends a rush of anger through your body! Suddenly, all that you learned at church becomes instantaneously replaced by, "Let me get him!"

However, once you spend more time with God, He will allow you to see what Satan and his demons are planning. You can pray, calm down, and begin to see the situation or perhaps the irritating coworker as a ploy arranged by Satan to pull you further from Christ. Imagine the frustration it would cause Satan if every time he kept sending people filled with contempt your way, you kept praying for them and demonstrating Christ's goodness. You may have to start looking for people to pray for because annoying people might no longer appear in your life! Hee-hee!

Jesus states:

> You have heard that it was said, "Love your neighbor and hate your enemy." But I tell you, love your enemies and pray for those who persecute you, that you may be children of your Father in heaven. He causes his sun to rise on the evil and the good, and sends rain on the righteous and the unrigheous. (Matthew 5:43–45 NIV)

We need to teach our children to pray for those who intentionally mistreat them and others, because they are victims of Satan's demonic corruption. Anytime we are placed among evil, we have an opportunity to awaken a deceived individual by demonstrating the goodness of Christ. We need to pray for God to give us strength to forgive and courage to deliver people from the grasp of Satan. Satan attempts to use people that he has deceived to cause us to hold bitterness and anger toward them. Since we are God's children, Satan wants to corrupt our souls with malice and an inability to forgive so that God will not forgive us.

Jesus states:

> For if you forgive other people when they sin against you, your heavenly Father will also forgive you. But if you do not forgive others their sins, your Father will not forgive your sins. (Matthew 6:14–15 NIV)

Train your children about this technique that Satan uses against us by demonstrating forgiveness in your life. Explain that the real war that is raging is not between each of us but between spiritual forces, and teach them how the power of prayer allows the Holy Spirit to fight this battle on our behalf. Our role is to become more like Jesus in every situation so that those who are deceived by Satan will marvel at the goodness of Christ and desire to know Him too!

Then I heard a loud voice in heaven say:

"Now have come the salvation and the power and the kingdom of our God, and the authority of his Messiah. For the accuser of our brothers and sisters, who accuses them before our God day and night, has been hurled down. They triumphed over him by the blood of the Lamb and by the word of their testimony; they did not love their lives so much as to shrink from death. Therefore rejoice, you heavens and you who dwell in them! But woe to the earth and the sea, because the devil has gone down to you! He is filled with fury, because he knows that his time is short." (Revelation 12:10-12 NIV)

Pruning Produces Fruit

Most people probably think that they don't know anyone that would go to Hell. In our little minds, that is only for the worst of the worst. Yet, God sees things differently.

> Or do you not know that wrongdoers will not inherit the kingdom of God? Do not be deceived: Neither the sexually immoral nor idolaters nor adulterers nor men who have sex with men nor thieves nor the greedy nor drunkards nor slanderers nor swindlers will inherit the Kingdom of God. (1 Corinthians 6:9–10 NIV)

> The acts of the flesh are obvious: sexual immorality, impurity and debauchery; idolatry and witchcraft; hatred, discord, jealousy, fits of rage, selfish ambition, dissensions, factions and envy; drunkenness, orgies, and the like. I warn you, as I did before that those who live like this will not inherit the Kingdom of God. (Galatians 5:19–21 NIV)

Though we have sinned and fall short of the glory of God, we can still make the commitment to stay attached to Christ and be led by the Spirit. When we allow God to prune our lives and remove some things, our lives can become more fruitful. There is a power that comes when we let go of the sinful things in our lives and become more connected to Christ. When God begins to make changes to our hearts, there is boldness and a God confidence that rises up, and believers start to become fearless because we can actually feel that our Father is *God*!

CHAPTER 4

"If You Remain in Me and I in You"

Part 2: The War
Summary

Jesus states:

> I AM THE VINE; YOU ARE THE BRANCHES. IF YOU
> REMAIN IN ME AND I IN YOU, YOU WILL BEAR MUCH
> FRUIT; APART FROM ME YOU CAN DO NOTHING.
> (JOHN 15:5 NIV)

- Satan (Lucifer or the devil) was created by God to be an angel in heaven.

- Satan formed an alliance with some angels in heaven in the hopes of becoming more powerful than God.

- Satan and his demonic angels lost their place in heaven and were sent to earth.

- There is now a spiritual warfare that has developed.

- God is the winner of this war, but Satan is still fighting to take as many of God's children with him as possible.

- We must ensure that we do not become victims of Satan's deceptive plans. We must obey the Holy Spirit's instructions and align our souls with God's will.

- Studying God's Word and praying gives us knowledge and wisdom concerning Satan's plans of attack in our lives and the lives of our children.

- God can give us the strength to overcome those attacks. His Word gives us instructions as to how to handle strategies of the devil.

- Being fully committed to growing closer to Christ gives us a power that Satan cannot defeat!

CHAPTER 4

"If You Remain in Me and I in You"

Part 3: Spiritual Maturity

Jesus states:

> I AM THE VINE; YOU ARE THE BRANCHES. IF YOU
> REMAIN IN ME AND I IN YOU, YOU WILL BEAR MUCH
> FRUIT; APART FROM ME YOU CAN DO NOTHING.
> (JOHN 15:5 NIV)

Spiritual Maturity Takes Time

Remember when I said that I believed the Spirit of God gave me three words: time, awareness, and discipleship? As we devote more time to God, we become aware of God, the world, and our mission to help our children and others get closer to Christ. This time with our Father builds spiritual maturity, and spiritual maturity is obtained by a renewing of our mind.

> Do not conform to the pattern of this world, but be transformed by the renewing of your mind. Then you will be able to test and approve what God's will is–his good, pleasing and perfect will. (Romans 12:2 NIV)

That scripture shows us how our souls must be aligned to God's will.

Each of us should always strive to reach spiritual maturity so that we have the proper tools to train our children. You may be asking, "How do I know if I am spiritually mature?" Well, you can easily find the answer to that question by evaluating the quality of time that you spend with God each day, your awareness of the spiritual things (godly or satanic) happening within your daily environment, and how focused you are on helping others get closer to Christ (discipleship).

And you can also simply ask yourself this question, "How do I handle obstacles?"

Oftentimes, the way in which we handle situations may determine how close we have gotten to Christ. Thankfully, the way in which I approach a difficult situation is vastly different than the way I would have years ago. We should begin to see our growth by the fruit that is given to us through the Spirit.

But the fruit of the Spirit is love, joy, peace, forbearance, kindness, goodness, faithfulness, gentleness and self-control. Against such things there is no law. (Galatians 5:22–23 NIV)

We obtain the ability to demonstrate these areas of the Spirit in our lives by reading the Word, spending more time with Christ, by working through our trials, and by allowing the Holy Spirit to gradually transform our souls to look the way God intended.

Spiritual Structures Develop Spiritual Maturity

No one can boast and say he or she is more spiritual than another, because no one can be spiritual without the Spirit of God. It is not ours to give to ourselves, but it is a gift from our Father in Heaven. I am not able to give myself peace or more faith, but the structures (spending time with God or what will be referenced as Vine time) that I set in place daily will put me in the right position to receive those blessings from God. Once we become Christians, some of us crawl toward Jesus, some walk, some jog, and others sprint. I have done all those, including running so fast toward God that I ran out of energy and then felt as though I was forever out of the race. God allows many chances. If you are breathing and have understanding, you have the ability to pick up right where you are and begin your walk closer toward His loving arms, all while carrying your children with you.

If we structure our lives with the sincere intent to get closer to our Father, He will help us. If we are not spending time in the presence of God, our level of spirituality gets confined, and the enemy has a greater ability to consume our children and us. The devil wants us to feel inadequate as Christians so that we will give up trying to live righteously. Don't let him confuse you like I have in my lifetime. Some days, I made a lot of mistakes, but God still loved me. Every day I had the ability to repent, learn a new lesson, and ask Jesus to strengthen me in my weak areas. God knows every mistake that we will make in our lives; yet, only He can take them and turn them into good!

And we know that in all things God works for the good of those who love him, who have been called according to his purpose. (Romans 8:28 NIV)

We must stay vigilant of the fact that God is our Higher Authority. That should be our first conscious mind-set of the day, and all things that happen within our day should fall under the realm of that statement. However, oftentimes, we allow our little world, which seems so big, to overshadow that most powerful Christian mind-set. That is exactly what Satan wants so that he can place doubt, confusion, and worry upon our lives. Our lives are so busy–that's why it's important to self-assess whether we are focused upon our relationship with Jesus, our growth as a Christian, and training our children properly. Demanding schedules can sometimes sneak up on us, so reevaluating our structural time with God must be a priority. We may need to renew or strengthen our focus upon

Him, so that the Spirit of God will place us in the right Christian mind-set to parent our children.

Parental Christian Mind-Sets

Before you proceed in this book, I would like for you to answer some questions. If you are married, please complete this questionnaire apart from your spouse. When answering the questions, please be as truthful as possible and make your answers strictly based upon how you think or the actions you take. If married, please do not base your answers on the thoughts or the actions of your spouse. This is your self-assessment. Afterward, each of you will average your individual totals separately. At the end of the survey, you will be given general information about the possibility of your current parental Christian mind-sets. I pray that by the time you and your spouse complete this book, your answers will start to align for the better. I also pray that single parents will become even more convinced to pursue Christ, thereby creating a generational breakthrough! Please don't judge one another or harbor any guilt, because where we are today in no way determines where God plans to take us. As long as we're living, let's plan to keep growing closer to Jesus!

Please read and complete this entire exercise because it will provide such clarity in your daily lives, and soon you can defeat some of Satan's tactics and schemes that he is planning against you and your children.

Parental Survey	Strongly Disagree	Disagree	Neutral	Agree	Strongly Agree
Time			Category	Total	
1. I attend church or Bible study almost weekly.	1	2	3	4	5
2. I require my children to study their Bibles, pray, and worship daily. (For younger children, I do this with them daily.)	1	2	3	4	5
3. I discuss God, Jesus, or the Holy Spirit with my child daily.	1	2	3	4	5
4. My children know or have observed that I study my Bible, pray, and worship daily.	1	2	3	4	5
5. When I need to make major decisions in my life, I DO NOT consult others before Christ.	1	2	3	4	5
Awareness			Category	Total	
6. I DO NOT allow my kids to listen to most secular music.	1	2	3	4	5
7. In most cases, children belong in a Christian school or should be homeschooled if possible.	1	2	3	4	5
8. Shows that are made for kids should be monitored by parents.	1	2	3	4	5
9. I pray for my children's relationship with God more than any other aspect of their lives.	1	2	3	4	5
10. I discuss life after death with my children without a cause.	1	2	3	4	5
Discipleship			Category	Total	
11. Most of my conversations with my friends are spiritually based.	1	2	3	4	5
12. I actively look for opportunities to bless others.	1	2	3	4	5
13. My children WOULD NOT say that I prefer them to make good grades more than being kind to others.	1	2	3	4	5
14. I teach my children to forgive and pray for those who mistreat them.	1	2	3	4	5
15. My children will often see me demonstrate God's love to people by sharing the gospel, praying with them, or by acts of service.	1	2	3	4	5
Thank you for investing the time to discover where you are on this spiritual parenting journey. Once you uncover your results, if applicable, review them with your spouse.	Numerical Average	Parental Christian Mindset			
Add your 3 category totals and divide the sum by 15. Put the average in Box 1. Look on the following pages for your numerical result range and record your Parental Christian Mindset in Box 2.	Box 1	Box 2			

Parental Survey	Strongly Disagree	Disagree	Neutral	Agree	Strongly Agree
Time			**Category**	**Total**	
1. I attend church or Bible study almost weekly.	1	2	3	4	5
2. I require my children to study their Bibles, pray, and worship daily. (For younger children, I do this with them daily.)	1	2	3	4	5
3. I discuss God, Jesus, or the Holy Spirit with my child daily.	1	2	3	4	5
4. My children know or have observed that I study my Bible, pray, and worship daily.	1	2	3	4	5
5. When I need to make major decisions in my life, I DO NOT consult others before Christ.	1	2	3	4	5
Awareness			**Category**	**Total**	
6. I DO NOT allow my kids to listen to most secular music.	1	2	3	4	5
7. In most cases, children belong in a Christian school or should be homeschooled if possible.	1	2	3	4	5
8. Shows that are made for kids should be monitored by parents.	1	2	3	4	5
9. I pray for my children's relationship with God more than any other aspect of their lives.	1	2	3	4	5
10. I discuss life after death with my children without a cause.	1	2	3	4	5
Discipleship			**Category**	**Total**	
11. Most of my conversations with my friends are spiritually based.	1	2	3	4	5
12. I actively look for opportunities to bless others.	1	2	3	4	5
13. My children WOULD NOT say that I prefer them to make good grades more than being kind to others.	1	2	3	4	5
14. I teach my children to forgive and pray for those who mistreat them.	1	2	3	4	5
15. My children will often see me demonstrate God's love to people by sharing the gospel, praying with them, or by acts of service.	1	2	3	4	5
Thank you for investing the time to discover where you are on this spiritual parenting journey. Once you uncover your results, if applicable, review them with your spouse.	**Numerical Average**	**Parental Christian Mindset**			
Add your 3 category totals and divide the sum by 15. Put the average in Box 1. Look on the following pages for your numerical result range and record your Parental Christian Mindset in Box 2.	**Box 1**	**Box 2**			

Worldly Christian Parental Mindset	Unaware Christian Parental Mindset	Foundational Christian Parental Mindset	Structured Christian Parental Mindset	Highly Structured Christian Parental Mindset
1.00 – 2.79	2.80 – 3.00	3.01 – 3.80	3.81 – 4.79	4.80 – 5.00
This type of parent may attend church a few Sundays here and there. You may also state that one doesn't need to attend a church to have a relationship with God. Being kind to people may give you a sense of heavenly security. Someone probably encouraged you to read this book, which I pray will be a blessing to you. You may place a higher value on the things of the world, and less about God's plan for your life. There's possibly a limited amount of Bible study or prayer time set by you. Perhaps you occasionally bless your food or teach your children a nightly prayer; yet, that is likely the extent of your godly talk. Socially, you may not be comfortable with people discussing God or spirituality with you. If your mind has been focused on how to live more comfortably within this world, you avoid placing much thought on the after-life. Your top definition of success for your children probably includes making good grades and becoming financially stable. You likely socialize with like-minded people because you see them as non-judgmental and logical. God is waiting!	This type of parent likely attends church occasionally. You perhaps realize that God should be important in your life; but, you may feel spiritually disconnected. Life might be a distraction and can lead you feeling overwhelmed. When you attend church, it could possibly be for the sake of your children. Hurt feelings may have placed many barriers between you and others and stunted your growth with God. Your main focus may be upon your own capabilities, leading you to place less thought on God's intercessions within your life. You may read your Bible periodically but are most likely uncomfortable discussing spirituality with others. Thinking about the ways Satan is trying to reach your children is probably a rare occurrence. Due to the likelihood that social status is a priority for you, you may have a lenient parenting style-- Thus you would prefer that your child has (within reason) what is needed for them to be socially accepted and happy. Go ahead and commit to daily Bible studying and prayer time! You will start to enjoy it!	You may have grown up with at least one parent or guardian attending church with you. You believe in God and believe in praying. However, you might find yourself repeating some old habits, which could lead to feeling disconnected from God at times. Due to certain circumstances and your foundation, you likely return to Christ; yet, may find yourself repeating the patterns again. You probably monitor what your kids are able to do to an extent but sometimes give in to the temptations of the world and allow them to take part in things that you are aware they shouldn't. Deep down, you may feel that you should strengthen your relationship with Christ, but sometimes can't figure out how to exactly start the process. Perhaps you feel it's easier just to stay where you are at times. Don't allow yourself to give in to those thoughts. Though you may have previously started a new process by setting a time to pray or read your Bible, but due to the bustling of life, you neglected your structure again. God is still waiting on you to lean on Him. Journaling and reflecting upon the times when you were more dedicated to God along with recreating your discipline might be all it takes to remain convicted and move you and your children even closer to Christ. Let your children see Him being the first priority to you!	I would gather that you attend church regularly. You possibly think about the ways Satan is trying to reach your children. This causes good boundaries and restrictions to be put in place. Your children may see you as a little strict, but as long as you develop a high level of communication, they will understand your reasoning. Remain humble, but know that since you likely have a deep relationship with Christ, this gives you the ability and the responsibility to be one of our Lord's disciples. You are probably already serving in some capacity at church or elsewhere. You love being in the presence of other Structured or Highly Structured Christians, but God equips us to be an encouragement and help lead others to Jesus. That means you may need to make some new friends. Ask God to help you be a light to others and train your children to become His disciples!	Thankfully, God is probably the head of your life; however, how you communicate with your children can affect how they view the church, God, and the world. In an effort to keep your children on the right path, you have probably placed a lot of restrictions upon them. It may be likely that you are seen as perfect. Once freedom arises, some young adult children of Highly Structured parents may rebel against their structured past lifestyles and give up trying to live up to the perfectionism, thereby turning from God for a period of time. While they are growing, seek guidance from God to learn how to balance life with Christianity. You may need to mentally release some of your power to God. Make sure your child understands that you made mistakes. Keeping in mind the appropriate age of your child, discuss your mistakes. Be forgiving like God forgives us. Allow your child to grow. Train them on the values early so that you may be able to release a little of the strictness later. Keep the foundation of prayer, Bible study, and worship, but create a fun "Life in the Vine." Enjoy life without becoming "worldly". Spend a lot of time talking to your children in a fun and relaxing way. Make sure they know that you are proud of them. I commend you for being aware that God must be the priority in your life and the lives of your children. Pray and ask God to guide and direct you so that you can parent in a way that teaches your children to learn and enjoy their daily structures!

This questionnaire was developed to offer insight into your parental Christian mind-set. Match your score range to the corresponding mind-set. Also notice your range to see if you are close to the adjusting category. If so, read it as well. Oftentimes people may shift between categories. Now review your category and see how it may depict some of your current views, mental thoughts, and/or actions.

Remember, parents may cross between parental Christian mind-set categories, so please review the category (Time, Awareness, and Discipleship) to see the areas that your total was the least. Ask God to reveal to you whatever He may want you to gather from the questionnaire, and journal your thoughts because Satan will not want you to remember any of it.

No matter which category fits you best, and no matter how many structures you set in place within your home, as parents our relationship with God determines it all. The godly structures that you begin to form each day are there so you have time to build your relationship with Jesus. He is the Master and can protect your children from things that you don't even know are headed their way. So put all your trust in Him, and let Him guide your steps. No child is beyond saving, because no circumstance is bigger than God. Increase your reliance upon Him and less on self. Remain faithful, and He will intercede like you wouldn't believe!

> Set your minds on things above, not on earthly things. (Colossians 3:2 NIV)

Think about your daily encounters with the Lord and the impact you are having on the spiritual development of your children. It is so important for us to spend time with God and implement our individual Spirit-led changes, so that we can grow closer to Christ, help save others, and become aware of Satan's tricks. Making time daily for God shields us from the devil and creates a greater awareness of the spiritual forces surrounding our daily lives. To demonstrate the cleverness of Satan, please read the skit called "Living outside the Bubble." As you read about this mother and son's morning, jot down in the appropriate boxes ways in which you noticed Satan was attacking this mother and son in each of the five categories. After you record your observations in the boxes, compare them to the "Detail Pages" following the skit. If you are married, please work on this together.

Devaluing & Corrupting the Sanctity of Marriage	Creating a Vice (Bad Habit)	Deception	Gossiping	Forgiveness

The skit is called "Living Outside the Bubble"

The characters in this story are:
Lucy: "The Foundational Christian Mind-Set" mom
Little Johnny: Lucy's eight-year-old son
Allison: The coworker
Barbara: Lucy's non-Christian friend

The scene starts off in Lucy and Little Johnny's home and then transitions to the car.

3, 2, 1, action.

Narrator. While Little Johnny is eating his fruity puffy cereal, Lucy is watching a typical morning news program. The meteorologist states the program will return after the break. A thirty-second seductive commercial about a new reality TV show appears that seems to be filled with many young people engaged in erotic activities in pools and bedrooms. They seem to be really enjoying themselves. Lucy sees the commercial but ignores it because she doesn't watch those types of shows. Little Johnny doesn't ignore it.

Lucy. Hurry and finish eating, I have to get you to school early because I am providing the opening statements during the morning meeting at work.

Narrator. She is slightly nervous about the meeting but is very proud of her job and the fact that she will provide the opening for the second time. Since it is taking him so long to finish his breakfast, she decides to check her emails.

Lucy. Wow!

Narrator. She notices an email that has a 50 percent off coupon for her favorite online store. When Little Johnny heard her yell, it startled him a bit.

Little Johnny. What is it, Mom?

Lucy. My favorite store is having an online sale today!

Little Johnny. Oh.

Narrator. He is completely unconcerned by the shopping thing.

Lucy, *sadly she states.* It's a great coupon, but since we are in so much debt and don't really need any new clothes, I better not buy anything. Plus, we don't have much money in the checking account. Oh, wait! I did however just receive a new credit card that I was saving for an emergency. I'm going to put it in my purse just in case I have an opportunity to browse the website during break. Who knows? I may find something that we really need.

Narrator. She runs into the bedroom, grabs the credit card from a drawer and sticks it inside her purse, and then they rush out the door. The two of them get into the car and head toward his school. Lucy turns on the radio. While driving she begins to think to herself.

Lucy. I know I should probably listen to contemporary Christian music or something while he is in the car, but I love this station. Also the commentators on this station are so funny and really put me in a good mood prior to going to work. I know the song that is playing is somewhat inappropriate, but Little Johnny is only eight years old. He isn't paying attention to any of the words; when he is older I will start to listen to Christian music.

Narrator. While smiling at Johnny in the review mirror, she bops around in her seat to the tune and taps her fingers to the beat. He smiles back because he loves to see his mom having a good time. Johnny recognizes a few of the bad words in some of the songs from the older kids at school. While driving down the road, Little Johnny sees a sexually explicit image of a woman on a billboard advertising a product. (For which the marketer had to really go out of the way to make a connection between this woman and the product.) Lucy hears a rather vulgar song come on the radio, so she turns it all the way down and decides to call her coworker, Allison.

Lucy. Good morning Allison. Are you ready for the meeting?

Allison. Oh yeah, I was just getting ready to call you. A couple of us were just discussing the last time you provided the opening for a meeting. You seemed just a little tongue-tied. So we decided to take that pressure off you. How about I provide the opening today?

Lucy, *feeling embarrassed.* Really? Why didn't you guys say anything to me after the last meeting?

Allison. Oh, cause it was no big deal really. You already have so much on your plate anyway. You don't need to worry about speaking at the meetings too.

Lucy. Okay … thanks."

Allison. Okay, bye, see ya in a bit.

Narrator. Lucy is feeling humiliated. Little Johnny is watching her from the backseat.

Little Johnny. Mom, did she make you mad?

Narrator. Lucy didn't want to concern him.

Lucy. No, honey, it's just work stuff.

Narrator. Lucy's phone rings, and it's her best friend Barbara (the non-Christian). Lucy forgot that she had just told Johnny she was fine, so she begins to yell and complain about Allison and the team at work.

Barbara. I know you are always trying to do the Christian thing, but I would give them a piece of my mind during the opening statement. When I was finish with them, they would all be calling on Jesus.

Narrator. Lucy gets Barbara off the phone. As she pulls toward the school drop-off line, the anger and insecurity starts to build. She looks at Little Johnny and tries to smile, but he could see the sadness in her eyes.

Lucy. You can expect a lot of new clothes coming your way, buster. With the type of morning I am having, I plan to put a ton on that credit card right after my lunch break.

Narrator. It is only 7:40 a.m.

The end.

Detail Pages

Compare your written results to the following detail pages. Pray and ask God to uncover ways in which Satan has been attempting to affect you and your children. Write in your journal anything that is revealed to you, and pray for direction to overcome the enemy's tactics.

Devaluing and Corrupting the Sanctity of Marriage in the Minds of the Youth

During the commercials at breakfast, Johnny is exposed to sexually alluring material that included young people engaged in promiscuous types of behavior. He also viewed the sexy pose of the woman on the billboard while on his way to school. How often does Satan find a way to present this type of information to our children? Satan's plan is for Johnny to develop sinful ideas about how he should view women and relationships from these images and to then get him to act upon those ideas and maybe even encourage his friends to do the same. Poor Lucy has been completely unaware of the numerous exposures throughout Johnny's life. Though she doesn't watch those types of shows, the unsuitable information has been reaching Johnny through many types of sources throughout his life. It is just starting to take shape and is planting a tiny seed within his mind that states promiscuity is exciting, expected, and accepted in our society. Though Johnny may not know what promiscuity means at this age, he knows what it looks like. Lucy doesn't know that her son is under attack by Satan. Most of our children are under the same attack. By viewing these images, what thoughts and ideas have our kids contemplated? Once Johnny becomes a teen, might he choose a lifestyle opposite that of a Christian?

One of Satan's plans of attack is to introduce to our kids socially or worldly acceptable images, in order to entice them into the world of pornography. This increases their desires to act out what they are viewing, and thus they often develop an addiction to this behavior. If by chance they decide to one day get married, Satan has already created the foundation that leads to adultery. If adultery doesn't happen in the physical form, the mental effects of pornography can destroy both their marriage and their relationships with our Lord. Pornography is a major priority to Satan because it can lead to sexual violence, sex-trafficking, experimentation between opposite sexes, and cause many other sexual and mental disorders. Most people begin to view pornography by the time they reach their teens. There are many studies that demonstrate the emotional damage that pornography causes marriages, some of which include: it becomes an addiction, can decrease sexual satisfaction with the marital partner due to desensitization, and it causes an emotional disconnect with the spouse. The significant other often feels insecure, and it is an abomination in the eyes of God.

Jesus states:

> "You have heard that it was said, do not commit adultery. But I tell you that anyone who looks at a woman lustfully has already committed adultery with her in his heart." (Matthew 5:27–28 NIV)

Due to a lack of discussion of this topic, Little Johnny may decide to choose an alternative lifestyle to that of a Christian; this would cause Lucy to cry and pray many nights for her son's return to Christ. Like so many Christian parents, she may be left wondering how this happened: "God, did I not take him to church? Did I not strive to lead by example?" As a parent, one of the steps Lucy needed to add was to pray for spiritual guidance to watch for Satan's roaming, and then add the biblical training and structures to Johnny's life. The definition of train is to instruct, teach, coach, tutor, educate, and drill. Without training, Satan can use this sexual immorality attack and many others on our youngsters to conquer and devour them.

> Be self-controlled and alert. Your enemy the devil prowls around like a roaring lion looking for someone to devour. (1 Peter 5:8 NIV)

Seek God's direction when handling this topic and make sure it is addressed at the appropriate times. Now, it's time to honor God's Word and regain what Satan thought he possessed.

Recreate the Sanctity of Marriage

Parents, we have to really understand that our children are sexually curious at very early stages of their lives. Just as children learn to walk and talk, they are also trying to learn about their bodies and that of the opposite sex. This curiosity may even begin by the time they are preschoolers. Typically by the time they reach regular school age, many have begun to combine their sexual knowledge with that of their peers to form a portrayal of sexual conduct derived from the views of our society. Most children know about sex prior to their parents deciding to *have the talk*. Kids are exposed to sex in many ways, and it is being taught to them by their friends or the internet. They are already visualizing sexual acts earlier than you can even imagine. It is difficult for a parent to realize this, but it is true. We have to first become honest with ourselves. Whether we are using all the precautionary steps to protect them from images, enrolling them in Christian schools, homeschooling, or sending them to church, they will be exposed to sexual content. With all the temptations available, the only real shield that can tame this desirable temptation until marriage is the Spirit of God. Through biblical teachings, our young ones must realize that once they accept Jesus as their savior, their sacred bodies will become "temples of God." This is where the "Spirit of God" dwells.

> Flee from sexual immorality. All other sins a man commits are outside his body, but he who sins sexually sins against his own body. Do you not know that your bodies are temples of the Holy Spirit, who is in you, whom you have received from God? You are not your own; you were bought at a price. Therefore honor God with your bodies. (1 Corinthians 6:18–20 NIV)

Satan is our "Enemy to the Temple." He wants to use perverse sexual activity as a way to contaminate "God's temples." Our children must know that they are made in the image of God and are created to become sacred temples that embrace the Spirit of our Father in Heaven. It is the same Spirit that created the world and that raised Jesus from the dead. Satan is on a mission to defile all of God's temples! So, parents, if you have had a nonchalant type of mind-set concerning sex prior to marriage, it is time to pray for a revelation. I have heard many Christians state, "Sex should be between two consenting adults who love and respect one another." However, this statement is incorrect because sex should be between a man and a woman who are joined through a godly union (called marriage) who are committed to spending the rest of their lives together.

Now let's say your child has already committed a sin such as premarital sex; forgive him or her, pray for him or her, pray for guidance, and teach him or her the Word of God. Explain the definition of repentance, and once they repent, make sure that they forgive themselves and let go of the guilt.

> If we confess our sins, he is faithful and just and will forgive us our sins and purify us from all unrighteousness. (1 John 1:9 NIV)

Parents, we too must be gracious and forgiving. The continuation of that verse reminds us of our own transgressions.

> If we claim we have not sinned, we make him out to be a liar and his word is not in us. (1 John 10 NIV)

So, let's be compassionate but firm when training our children.

Though it is imperative that we focus diligently on reducing the types of negative exposures available to the youth, we must be aware that Satan has carved out a strategic plan that makes it extremely challenging to prevent all those unwanted exposures. Even if our children are not exposed within their homes, Satan has set up many other ways for them to receive undesirable messages.

Within the home, we can block many inappropriate materials, but rarely all. As you saw in Lucy's case, she was watching a morning news program when the show was interrupted by a racy reality show advertisement. Proper communication, prayer, and biblical guidance with our young ones can prepare them to stand firm against abhorrent temptations prompted by friends or any other forms of influence. Parents should always observe their children and make a mental note of sins that have a positive portrayal in society and among their peers; then, parents should find an appropriate but tranquil time to casually discuss what they saw using the Bible as their reference.

Children do not want to feel as though they are in a classroom when issues like these are brought to their attention. In most cases, the conversations need to be relaxed and can often be while cooking together, driving in the car, playing a board game, or even while enjoying the outdoors. Though not everyone has the time for this, in our home each child has his or her own parental alone time daily. This alone time started at birth and will continue as long as they live in our home. We use it to watch TV, talk, tell jokes, play a game, or just be silly. Many of our most important godly talks have come out of those times. The kids are not even aware that we just fought Satan! They just know we had so much fun together.

These discussions should have an "Oh, yeah, by the way" feel. In Johnny's case, age eight, Lucy will find time later in the day to discuss with Johnny the reasons why those shows are inappropriate. Conversations can often start with, "I saw a commercial this morning where these young adults were kissing and lying together in beds. Did you see that? Have your friends ever talked about those types of things? I don't even think they were married, do you? Have I ever told you what God says about marriage?" Later, read a Bible verse about what God says concerning marriage and explain that those young people in that dating reality show were not demonstrating God's love.

> He who finds a wife finds what is good and receives favor from the Lord.
> (Proverbs 18:22 NIV)

As Johnny gets older, other verses can be discussed with him, but it is good to start with something simple to encourage him that marriage is precious and should be honored. He needs to feel that what he viewed is not of God and does not glorify the type of love that God created for him to one day experience.

You see, though Satan has his plan, he is no match against our Savior and the power of God's Word. As years go by, I hope Lucy would continue to pray daily and find the appropriate times to bring up this topic often. If we combine this training with biblical truth and prayer, Satan's plans will be ruined! Over time as Johnny ages, he would eventually learn that society's acceptance of this sin is unacceptable in the eyes of God; thereby, it will become unacceptable to Johnny. So he will lovingly but boldly speak against sexual immoralities to his friends thus becoming, yep, one of God's disciples.

Downfall of Creating a Vice

A vice is best characterized as a bad habit. It is normally a practiced behavior that is considered wrong or immoral. People may sometimes think of vices in the worst possible way; however, some vices can appear to be harmless yet have detrimental effects on your spiritual growth. Did you notice a particular vice that Lucy had in the story? What can the devil do with a vice? If you were born or live outside that bubble, you likely have a couple of those sins that you have had to battle internally. Let me explain why it is so important to pray for a release of them. Many people use a vice or sin to help them overcome a particular feeling or situation. These vices often lead to an increased number of sins and a feeling of detachment from our Father in Heaven. Our vices are also observed by our children. This may sadly encourage them, once they become adults, to create their own vices to overcome negative emotions, thereby causing our offspring to feel detached from God, and the cycle continues on to the next generation.

Oftentimes, this is why we have so many substance abuse centers, weight management programs, debt counselors, and many other centers for handling addictive behavioral issues. Anytime Satan can take your worrisome feelings and cause you to replace them with a substance or a negative action in the hopes of regaining a positive emotion, you have been under his attack. Any positive emotion created by a sin will not remain and will only multiply your negative emotions and your number of sins. We will often have situations where we feel unappreciated, sad, lonely, insecure, or upset. However, we really can overcome all those emotions. Yet, instead of turning to Jesus, Satan wants us to use a sin for the solution. He knows that by doing this, we will reach for that vice each time until it becomes a habit and then becomes our label.

Say your habit when stressed is overeating; soon your new label may become obese. This tactic is accomplished in many ways: food deprivation to anorexic, overspending to broke, drinking to alcoholic, medication usage to drug addict, promiscuity to sex addict, or even something like shopping to a shopaholic (men, don't automatically start labeling your wives here). Once Satan has tricked you into believing that your vice has become your label, the mental detachment from God may start to take place. Satan will then be on a greater mission to consistently set up situations to take you deeper into your habit, leaving you numb and mentally convinced that you have been forever stamped with this new embarrassing label.

In Lucy's case, she was upset with her coworkers because they obviously thought that she could not adequately deliver the opening statements at the morning meeting. This feeling of humiliation caused mental insecurities to develop within Lucy. Instead of turning to Jesus for comfort, Lucy probably replays the conversation with Allison, which only fuels her anger. So she turns to her reliable vice—shopping. Ladies, you may be thinking, *Shopping is not bad, especially due to the fact that she had a 50 percent off coupon.* Remember that Satan wants to attack you and your family by whatever means is necessary. During the moment that Lucy felt hurt, she decided to replace those negative feelings with her vice—shopping.

You may now be shouting (especially if you are a woman), "If shopping is a sin, I'm in trouble!" Let me prevent all the moms from closing this book or abandoning this course. Shopping is not a sin, but it became Lucy's vice. Lucy stated she was already in debt.

> The rich rule over the poor, and the borrower is slave to the lender. (Proverbs 22:7 NIV)

Now, she will significantly add to that debt only because she did not allow the Spirit of God to give her the strength to handle this situation and rid her of the insecurities. Not only has it become her vice, but staying in debt can restrict her willingness to tithe, be generous, or have financial peace. Remember this: any positive emotion created by a sin will not remain and will only multiply your negative emotions and your number of sins.

Regardless of how Lucy is allowing one conversation to have a negative impact on her spiritual peace, one of the most important things to Satan is attacking Little Johnny, because his goal is to create more corruption for the next generation. Lucy is unintentionally training him to replace negative emotions with a sin. There will be many times in Lucy's life that she will feel hurt, upset, or sad. So how many times will her son see her use a vice to counteract her failure to adequately cope with the situations? Let's just say that if she doesn't learn how to make Jesus Lord over all situations, it will be many times.

Satan knows what she is capable of doing and what she is not. She will not use a vice like drugs or alcohol. I'm sure he already tried those during her lifetime. However, he has a plan for Little Johnny, if he can just get his mom to train him to create a vice, Satan can then use a vice to one day become Johnny's habit, and then later Little Johnny will believe that he has a new label. Lucy's "Christian" friends will be left wondering: "How did that once well-mannered cute little boy turn into an alcoholic, drug addict, or head toward a downward spiral out of control?" And her non-Christian friend Barbara will be left stating; "I told her there was no use in taking that boy to church."

Overcoming the Desire to Create a Vice

Using something to overcome a negative feeling is one of the easiest sins to commit in front of our children and not even realize it. Anytime we are faced with a challenging situation or consumed with emotions or thoughts that are difficult to tolerate, it's time to pray. Please don't get me wrong here; when we are having a bad day, it's okay to occasionally reward ourselves with something that is pleasurable, as long as the thing providing the pleasure is not a sin, doesn't cause future harm, and is not being used to temporarily fix the problem. Many vices become habitual solutions for an inadequate situation.

Now, I am not a doctor, but I know that certain chemicals in the brain are released during moments of pleasure (example, Serotonin and Dopamine). I believe that some people may have certain chemical imbalances that require medical treatments by physicians. If anyone is having severe issues with properly handling thoughts, he or she should seek medical assistance, spiritual counseling, and pray. However, many people may reach for stimulants (vices) to create a mood-enhancing alternative to a negative circumstance, which could have been handled by first seeking Jesus and asking for the Spirit of our Lord to intercede and provide peace and proper guidance in handling those emotions. God can deliver far greater benefit to our lives than any temporary solution provided by a vice. You can be victorious over this temptation. Later, in your journal moment, you will have the opportunity to profoundly reflect upon any vices small and large that you may feel are starting to have you in bondage.

Once you have observed the types of vices you have created, you can begin to pray for Jesus to release those strongholds. Be aware of the circumstances that caused you to feel led to reach for those temptations, and pray immediately for strength and self-control. We will discuss the fruit of the Spirit in detail later, but it's good to pray for an increase in these areas. Wisdom and knowledge are two gifts that God can anoint upon His children, but we also need the fruit of the Spirit to properly handle many negative areas of our daily lives.

> But the fruit of the Spirit is love, joy, peace, forbearance, kindness, goodness, faithfulness, gentleness and self-control. Against such things there is no law. (Galatians 5:22–23 NIV)

An elevation of the fruit of the Spirit can often lead to a dismissal of vices. I often pray and ask God to help me in the area of self-control. I loved sweets! When I felt hurt, disappointed, or frustrated, I would reach for sweets. God taught me that I was creating a vice. It wasn't good for me or for the *entire future* of my children. Remember, our vices may seem miniscule compared to the vices that Satan is attempting to bring forth in the lives of our children. So now I have learned to save the cheesecake for the occasional treat, not the occasional overcomer because only Jesus is our redeemer and overcomer!

Journal Moment (Vices)

I loathe vices because they can become extremely detrimental to our lives. They can keep us so chained that the joy of life can turn into a rare occurrence. It is time to get to know who God says you are, and demolish your mental thoughts involving Satan's label that he wants to place upon you. First, you have to realize your vices, and then allow God to re-create your joy by helping you release them from your lives.

When I was attempting to overcome my vices and praying to God for a release, they seemed to have gotten worst. I refused to stop calling upon Jesus. I wrote in my journal about how much I was struggling. I now believe Satan was attacking me more aggressively, but God caused Satan's stronghold to convince me to never return to that lifestyle. It also brought forth a new level of humbleness inside me because I learned that all my strength is in God.

Now I live in the peace and glory of my Father and turn to Him for all of life's pain and disappointments. He loves us so much and is capable of removing every hurt. God can provide an indescribable peace within us because Jesus is our peace.

As a form of acknowledgment and healing, list in your journal some ways that you believe Satan is trying to attack you and your children by the use of vices. The definition of a noun is a person, place, thing, or idea. Satan uses each of those to attack us. Think deeply about that definition and list where you and your child might be under attack. Now, think about how you handle or respond to those attacks.

If you need some assistance, here are some questions that may allow you to begin:

- Which vices have you created?

- Which nouns cause you to reach for these vices?

- How does it negatively affect your walk with God?

- Have your children seen you partake of these vices?

- Have you included your children in the use of these vices?

- How might your vices have an effect on your children?

- How have you observed your children handling stress?

- What vices, if any, have you noticed your children starting to create? How do you think the Holy Spirit is leading you to help them overcome their particular vices before they escalate?

Deception

Deception comes in many forms. We may sometimes deceive others and ourselves, or Satan and others may sometimes deceive us! By now, I am sure that you have started to realize that Satan is truly working in our lives all the time, trying to gain access to our futures. I pray that you will begin to look upon small occurrences through each day and be able to say to Satan, "Oh, no you don't," then just call upon the glorious name, Jesus!

Let's talk about some of the areas of deception in the story.

- Lucy believes that adding new debt (during work hours) will relieve her of the emotional distress.

- Lucy lies to Little Johnny by telling him that she was not upset.

- Satan deceives Lucy by thinking that Little Johnny is not aware of the inappropriate music or the sexual material he is observing.

- Lucy allows Allison to cause her to doubt her very own capabilities, thereby creating insecurities.

If improperly addressed, deception can have lifelong effects. It causes hurt, pain, guilt, and distrust of others. It can be so harmful that some people never forgive others. We have to recognize deceptions in all forms. If someone leads you to believe you are incapable of achieving something, then reference this verse:

56

Jesus looked at them and said, "With man this is impossible, but with God all things are possible." (Matthew 19:26 NIV)

Satan may even try to use verses to deceive you. For instance, that verse didn't state that we will do all things; it stated that with God, all things are possible. God will choose the things that He wants to be possible for us to do. We must trust in God's decision to strengthen us to do what He wants us to accomplish.

One of the most prominent forms of deception is to lie. I have heard many parents tell "little white lies." I have also heard darker-skinned parents tell "little brown lies." By now you should be accustomed to my humor.

Sometimes lies are used as a means to prevent a negative response. Many lies occur to enhance a story or make a person feel valued or humorous. Oftentimes, people lie to prevent hurting someone's feelings or simply because it's difficult for them to say no to a specific question or invitation. Lies are often justified when they are used to make others feel good about themselves. Other lies are told to change the outcome of a situation or to avoid some type of conflict. Lastly, people may alter a story or event in the hopes of making it less embarrassing.

Regardless of the numerous reasons, all lies are a sin, and once you get closer to God, you will become bolder and will work toward refraining from deception. When I was a little girl, I thought it was a sin for me to even say the word *lie* in front of Grandma. My dear grandmother thought of that word as a curse word. If she was alive today, I would be punished for writing it so many times!

Many people are dishonest when giving a reason as to why they don't want to do something. God can give you the confidence to kindly say no when you can't or would not like to do something. You will feel okay afterward because your heart will be right with God. Practice kindly saying no without creating false excuses. You can learn to value your integrity and to detest deception.

I remember a time when a friend of mine and I were led to stop all "little white and brown lies." Well, we had to meet a business associate by 8:00 a.m. This associate was wearing an extremely bright-colored scarf; yet, the rest of her outfit had earthy-tone colors. The associate looked at us and said, "You two look so beautiful this morning." Well, since that scarf was standing out so much, I quickly replied, "Oh, thank you, and so do you. I *loooooovvvve* that scarf!"

After our associate left, my friend said, "Did you really *loooooovvvve* that scarf?"

I sadly thought, *No, I didn't. I didn't even like it.*" I had spent so many years trying to make others feel good that along the way I started lying for absolutely no reason. I didn't chase her down and say, "Hey, I really don't *loooooovvvve* or *like* your scarf!" I simply repented and asked God to make me aware of my deceptive traits and to help me stop being dishonest.

Later, when I had the urge to give a deceitful compliment, I would think of that scarf. Since women are such nurturers, I believe we suffer from this more often than men, but we must learn to just say, "Thank you" without the need to return a compliment. Thankfully, God has given me the capability to stop being deceptive.

You may be thinking, *Why is it so bad to tell a lie in the hopes of making others feel better about themselves?* The answer is simple; the Bible tells us not to be deceptive, and Satan uses all sin to not pull God farther from us, but to pull us farther from God. Satan is hovering just waiting to teach our children that it's okay to lie. You as the parent may be saying it's okay to lie in this situation, but Satan is saying it's also okay to be deceptive in all these situations too.

> The Lord detests lying lips, but he delights in people who are trustworthy.
> (Proverbs 12:22 NIV)

Remember, any form of deception may become habitual and when viewed by your children may be imitated. So if this is one of your sins, it's time to overcome it. I have seen parents tell "little white and brown lies" in front of their children and then punish their kids for cheating on a test or lying to them. Always remember to live out the life you want your children to live.

Parents, Let's Take an Oath Here

Moms: Say, "I declare that I will strive to tell the truth and nothing but the truth. I will no longer follow up a received compliment with a disingenuous compliment. I will kindly and respectfully say no when I don't want to do something without giving a false explanation."

Other Moms: Say, "I will not get offended if I give a compliment and don't receive one back from the same person. I will not feel offended if someone kindly says no to me if I have asked him or her to do something he or she does not desire. I will not talk about this person behind his or her back or hold *lifelong* grudges against him or her."

Dads: (Oh, you didn't think you all escaped this topic did you?) Say, "I will not lie to prevent my ego from being compromised. I will not lie to avoid a confrontation. Instead, I will boldly stand as a man of God asking God to give me courage to handle the situation. I will not allow past hurt or embarrassment to cause me to erroneously enhance a story. I will not embellish an event or a past sporting activity in order to gain more respect or honor among my peers!" (My husband said if men honor these oaths, they may no longer have anything to discuss! Hee-hee, pray for him.)

Seriously, throughout our day, there can be many times where deception can creep in to destroy. So please stay on guard! Your children must see you being honorable and trustworthy. When you make a mistake around them, repent to Jesus, tell them you made a mistake and explain it.

Musical Deception

Now let's take a moment to address Satan's deception concerning the type of music and lyrics in the songs of today. Many biblical scholars believe that when Satan, (a.k.a. Lucifer) was in heaven, he was a musician. Well, that sure would explain a lot, wouldn't it? Have you listened to some of the lyrics in today's music? I am saddened by the many musicians that are so talented, and yet, the day they sign those contracts, it's as though they were signing a contract with Satan himself. Their music quickly becomes perversely competitive. Though they're making more money, their clothes seem to disappear from their bodies. Some secular artists are constantly attempting to create music and videos that are viler and more corrupt than their predecessors.

They are victims of the ultimate levels of deception, so much so that when they receive an award, they begin to thank God for the success that was derived from sin. God gave them talents, but they didn't use them correctly. This often makes me think of what Satan said to Jesus in the wilderness:

> The devil led him [Jesus] up to a high place and showed him in an instant all the kingdoms of the world. And he said to Him, "I will give you all their authority and splendor, for it has been given to me, and I can give it to anyone I want to. So if you worship me, it will all be yours." Jesus answered, "It is written: Worship the Lord your God and serve Him only." (Luke 4:5–8 NIV)

Sadly, many young artists (musicians, dancers, choreographers, etc.) are not even aware that it is Satan that has led them to what they perceive as success in this world. Perceived success that is obtained by a growth of sin is not success at all. They have so much wealth because the devil recognizes the power of artistic expression such as music. He can use one musician to destroy many lives. These lyrics heard repetitively have a persuasive impact on the mind. It can seep into the thoughts and cause a personality shift. Due to earphones and many devices that kids possess, oftentimes parents are not even aware of the lyrics. Please understand that these songs can have a profound effect on our children. Pray for protection in the area of music, pray for the artists that are being deceived, and ask God to direct you in regard to handling this in your homes.

Fortunately, not all songs are harmful. Be wise and enjoy the many ways God blesses us with the talents that He has placed inside people. I commend the many artists that use their talents to bring a spiritual awakening to a generation. They will be blessed! The most powerful music lifts us spiritually and directs our hearts and minds to worship the Lord. Train your children early regarding the real joy of music.

If your children's little ears are already trained to enjoy inappropriate music, seek God for guidance. There are many types of Christian-based artists whose songs have similar sounds of secular artists but include godly messages.

Gossiping

Please reference these verses that pertain to gossiping: Proverbs 20:19, Psalms 141:3, Ephesians 4:29, Proverbs 16:28, Psalms 101:5, Proverbs 21:23.

What wasn't directly mentioned in the story, but you may have gathered was the fact that Allison, the coworker, negatively gossiped with other coworkers about Lucy's performance. This led to the last-minute decision to deny her the ability to provide the opening statement at the meeting. When you are not sure if what you are about to say is considered slandering, before you speak, ponder whether your words could benefit or hinder someone's relationship with God. Gossip is a major issue for people, especially women. We may have to make a conscious choice not to gossip. I don't know why this is such a struggle for some women, but we have to admit that it probably is for most. I sometimes wonder if this behavior began during the Old Testament days when husbands had multiple wives. I'm sure that wives began to exile themselves from the favorite wife. Can you imagine the tension, jealousy, and backstabbing that existed? This trait was probably taught early by mothers and was carried forth all the way into our generation.

Once we make the decision to stop this negative behavior, it is actually very freeing. As a woman, you may need to make an upfront statement to your female coworkers, family members, and friends letting them know that you have decided not to take part in gossiping any longer and advise them to do the same. This may mean that you have to excuse yourself from a few conversations. Tell them that just as you love them and are not willing to participate in a conversation condemning them, as a Christian, your feelings for another must be consistent. Young girls often learn this behavior from their mothers and begin to model it among their friends. It is not pleasing to God, and as parents, we need to remove it from our list of sinful behavioral traits.

Forgiveness

One of the most difficult things for people is to forgive those that mistreat them and their families. It will likely be a challenge for Lucy to forgive Allison and the other coworkers. I'm sure Satan is sending Lucy messages that sound just like a friend within her mind, "How dare they treat you that way? They obviously talked about you behind your back, and then waited to the last minute to reveal that you would not be giving the opening statement during the morning meeting! You worked so hard to prepare that message only to be ridiculed and left feeling like an outcast!"

You see, that's the way Satan responds. He never wants us to forgive because he knows that when we forgive, we are becoming more like Christ. Remember, in order for Christ to forgive us of our sins, we must forgive others. Parents, we must win this battle against Satan. Refuse to allow him to control your thoughts. Ask Jesus for strength in this area. Teach your children to pray for those who mistreat them, and explain that if someone deliberately persecutes them, it is, sadly, Satan working through that individual. Prayers are needed for any person that consciously attempts to ridicule or hurt others because he or she is blinded and doesn't fully understand the love of God.

In Lucy and Allison's case, we don't know if Lucy had a difficult time during the last morning meeting or not, but we do know that Allison could have handled the situation differently. Nevertheless, Lucy will pray for Jesus to help her forgive; she will stop replaying the conversation with Allison in her mind, and she will realize that she is not who Allison thinks she is. Lucy is who God says she is.

We are so important to God that He made sure that we knew it by the first book and the first chapter of the Bible.

> So God created mankind in his own image; in the image of God he created them; male and female he created them. (Genesis 1:27 NIV)

I hope Lucy and Little Johnny's story, "Living Outside the Bubble," opened your eyes to your own world. Satan is roaming for a reason. Begin to watch moments in your life closely. When you keep your eyes set on Jesus, you will receive guidance and revelation. Once you begin to pray over your household and receive guidance from the Lord, you will be amazed at how the Spirit will start to transform you, your household, and others who come into contact with you. Believe in God's power to not only overcome Satan's plans but to allow you and your family to become more than conquerors!

CHAPTER 4

"If You Remain in Me and I in You"

Part 3: Spiritual Maturity
Summary

Jesus states:

> I AM THE VINE; YOU ARE THE BRANCHES. IF YOU
> REMAIN IN ME AND I IN YOU, YOU WILL BEAR MUCH
> FRUIT; APART FROM ME YOU CAN DO NOTHING.
> (JOHN 15:5 NIV)

- Spiritual maturity is achieved when your mind has been renewed and your thoughts/actions begin to align more to the Word of God.

- Spiritual maturity is visible when we demonstrate the fruit of the Spirit in our daily lives (love, joy, peace, patience, kindness, goodness, faithfulness, gentleness, and self-control).

- No one should ever boast and say he or she is more spiritual than another. Spiritual maturity is only obtained by the Spirit of God.

- Do not condemn others for what you may perceive as being a lack of spirituality in their lives. Always demonstrate the fruit of the Spirit to others and pray for one another.

- When we increase our time with God, He increases our awareness, and our desire to be disciples. One of the most important areas of discipleship is with your spouse and children.

- Whether our parental mind-set is listed as worldly Christian, unaware Christian, foundational structured Christian, structured Christian, or highly structured Christian, we all have opportunities for growth and development.

- Our souls should consistently become more like Christ. We won't be fully converted until we are with our Father in Heaven. However, our spiritual growth within this world will help us stay connected to the Vine and be the light that leads our children and others to Christ.

- As you proceed through each day, pray for the Holy Spirit to guide your steps closer to Jesus and to help your family overcome the attacks caused by Satan and his demons. Teach your children that these attacks are often from Satan working through man.

- We must pray for those who are deceived by Satan and who consciously set out to hurt others because they are victims of Satan's strongholds and lack the full knowledge of our Father's love.

CHAPTER 4

"If You Remain in Me and I in You"

Part 4: Order in the House!

Jesus states:

> I AM THE VINE; YOU ARE THE BRANCHES. IF YOU
> REMAIN IN ME AND I IN YOU, YOU WILL BEAR MUCH
> FRUIT; APART FROM ME YOU CAN DO NOTHING.
> (JOHN 15:5 NIV)

Your Life

Please answer these questions to prepare your mind for the next topic.

- Describe how you would like your home life to be surrounding these very important topics.

    - Spiritually:

    - Emotionally:

    - Spouse:

    - Kids:

    - Home Environment:

- Is your home life in line with the way you envisioned it to be? If not, what are the ways that you previously attempted to make your life accurately align with your vision?

- If applicable, why do you believe that your reality did not adequately align with the way you envisioned your life to be?

- Do you believe that God's way of doing things will work better than the way you may have been previously living? If yes, how so?

- How do you believe that your life might be blessed if you maintained a closer connection to Christ?

- Are you willing to order your life; so, that you will have a greater ability to establish a firmer connection to Christ and make more time for your family?

Let's Get Our Houses in Order!

Do you remember when I first mentioned how I was attempting to write this book among the many other things that I had to do during the week? I was getting very overwhelmed. Though I no longer had my regular job, my life was still feeling a bit chaotic while attempting to complete the book along with my other responsibilities. As I was finalizing the first version of this book, I kept thinking, *It's not in order.* It felt like the Holy Spirit boldly stated within my mind, *"Oh, it will be in order!"* I didn't know what that meant until now. God was putting this book together to represent order. He wants complete order, not just in this book but in our everyday lives!

By now, you know how easy it is for Satan to just sneak in our homes through a small crack. Nevertheless, God gives us everything we need to overcome him and train our children to remain in the Vine. However, we must create time for God by creating order within our lives so that we can mentally receive all that the Holy Spirit wants to present to us. Think about it; there are 168 hours in a week. A majority of Christians probably attend church at least one hour a week, which is good! However, if you are not devoting time to God in your homes as well, you may not be equipping yourselves or your children with all the armor needed to stay connected to the Vine.

Say you have a child that is eighteen years old, and he or she only received information about God during church service for about one hour every week of their lives. By the time this child turned eighteen, he or she would have had 936 hours of godly information. On the other hand, let's just say that all their other time including sleep would have been devoted to the world. This would leave 156,312 hours of worldly time. We have seen through the lives of Lucy and Little Johnny what Satan can do by 7:40 a.m. And we wonder how people stray from the Lord? The sin in this world was created by Satan working through people and is designed to make us sin even more. Once you get that, you will realize the importance of running from sin until you are strong enough in Christ to face it and fight it!

The only way we obtain the type of strength that we need is through the Holy Spirit. Spending more time with God gives us a worldly detoxing, which is what God did with me when He called me to write this book. It became one of the greatest blessings I have received. My eyes have never been more opened to Christ. He trained me through a daily process of waking up each day with a mind renewal that all I needed to do was to rely upon Him. Some days I felt so overwhelmed with all the things that I needed to accomplish in a day that I had to stop and pray because once the feeling of anxiousness set in, I no longer felt that I was being led by God. This taught me to slow down and take inventory of my emotions and thoughts.

I thought, *God, how do people stay connected to Christ when they are working several jobs or raising children as single parents?* It was my moment of awakening. When we feel anxiety, we may quench the Holy Spirit or suppress the manifestation of the plans that He has for us, and a disorderly lifestyle often creates anxiousness.

> Do not be anxious about anything, but in every situation, by prayer and petition, with thanksgiving, present your requests to God. And the peace of God, which transcends all understanding, will guard your hearts and your minds in Christ Jesus. (Philippians 4:6–7 NIV)

God revealed to me that a disorderly lifestyle can be a major problem in our lives.

> But everything should be done in a fitting and orderly way. (1 Corinthians 14:40 NIV)

Many of our issues likely derived from chaotic environments. Satan doesn't want our finances, homes, or any part of our lives to be in order! For the devil to fulfill some of his plans, he needs disorder around us. This causes a decreased amount of focused godly time, distractions that lead to an inability to hear from the Holy Spirit and a lack of a desire to complete our purposes. Mental distress affects marriages, families, and our ability to focus on discipleship. Wow! I couldn't believe how I had been duped my entire life!

Order in Your Finances

One of the things that God wants His children to get a handle on is our finances. Numerous studies talk about the percentage of marriages that failed due to financial issues. Thankfully, God kept Saint and me together because we were always in debt. Even as we were tithing and giving, we remained in debt. God was helping us pay our bills, but we didn't know how to make wise spending choices. This is such a sad concept, but if I'm honest with myself, I think sometimes I began to think that since we were tithing, we should be able to spend how we wanted and wait for God to return the funds. I learned that God loves us, but He doesn't owe us anything. He blesses us because He loves us.

Through God's grace, He would still allow us to pay off some of our debt, but due to our careless spending habits, we would multiply the amount of debt that we paid off within months. One day, I believe God led me to sign us up for Dave Ramsey's Financial Peace University course. I talked it over with Saint, and we agreed to take the course. We loved the fact that Dave focused on tithing (10 percent of our income going to our church). We were already tithing, but that course taught us how to detest debt and how to budget our finances. I believe that God not only led us to that course to release us of debt but so that I could afford to stay home for a while and fulfill my calling to write this book. If we were still living the way we were previously, our chaotic spending habits would have placed me in a selfish mind-set preventing me from focusing on God's will but on my own will. That was just another example of how God was preparing us to answer "The Call."

If you are living a life full of debt, please obtain financial assistance and begin to experience the rewards of working toward being debt free. If you are not currently tithing, pray about it, and ask God to renew your mind and heart concerning tithing. God has more than proven Himself to us concerning the benefits of returning to God what is already His. You can ask almost any person who has been consistently tithing, and you will hear testimony after testimony about God's faithfulness. However, the rewards are icing on the cake because the real internal joy and peace will come from your obedience.

Clean Your House

The next area of our lives that has always created tension is our struggle to balance life with our ability to maintain a tidy home. Now God blessed us with our homes, so how did some of ours turn into messy globs of pandemonium? Confess it by saying, "Satan is the reason my house is a mess!" Whew! Don't you feel better? It's not our fault! It's just another scheme of his. However, now that we know this, we have to fix it. We don't want the devil and his demons anywhere near us and especially not in our homes! So the first step to getting our houses in order is to literally get our houses in order. Don't worry; Saint and I are trying to get organized too. If your environment is disorganized, it's time to clean it. Make it fun! Come together with your spouse, kids, family, and friends, and clean your home. Play powerful Spirit-uplifting music, have a cookout, and tell people that you are structuring your home to make time to visit with the Holy Spirit. Have a yard sale or, better yet, give away items and put signs out front that say, "Cleaning up 'cause the Holy Spirit has moved in, and Satan has moved out!" Try to have this task completed as soon as possible but no later than sixty days from the time that you are reading this. By the remarkable grace of God, He has led me to develop templates to help you organize your days. As you are working toward getting your finances in order and organizing your house, you can also begin the process of restructuring your time by formulating your personal dynamic plan that I believe the Holy Spirit will help you develop so that you can begin your orderly lifestyle.

Vine Time and Order

A few pastors at my church were discussing the impact it might make on our lives if we began to tithe our time to the Lord. So I began planning my days with an emphasis on tithing (10 percent) of my time to Him. Let me tell you, this has made a huge difference in my life and has been more of a blessing to me than you can even imagine! I see God in everyday occurrences so much clearer now. I hope to always be able to have this personal time with God on a daily basis.

Now remember, we are all different, and the Spirit has to lead us differently. The Spirit of God will lead those who have a relationship with Him to live righteously. Just like having our own fingerprints, our various life experiences also make our steps closer to Him uniquely different.

The one thing that I know for certain is that God wants us to make time for Him and that this time benefits our lives greatly. Not everyone should tithe (10 percent) of their time to the Lord on a weekly basis just because I stated it in this book. Your Vine time should be led by the Spirit of God. God may lead some of you to set aside 3 percent of your time or more than 10 percent for others. If you are feeling led to give God 3 percent of your time, then that may be hours more than what you are currently setting aside for Him on a weekly basis, so that's great! Be grateful for the Holy Spirit convicting you to make a new commitment to faithfully honor God with your time. As we all journey through this process, I believe that we will form good habits and routines that will lead us toward a new life filled with time set aside for God that comes as natural as breathing, and in return God will lead us to a life of true satisfaction and prosperity!

This is not just about setting aside time for God, but it is also about ordering and structuring your life so that you don't feel frenzied, overworked, overwhelmed, and stressed about accomplishing so much during the day. You don't want to add to your daily routine but organize it so that your days and life flow more smoothly.

When our lives are out of order, our kids often feel the tension that surrounds a disorderly lifestyle and environment. In our home, my tension would often escalate if Saint decided to rest from a hard day at work and watch TV. He would sometimes say, "I love you" as he placed a dirty dish next to me while I was washing the dishes. I thought, *If you love me, you would wash these dishes.* Satan didn't want me to think about how Saint provided for us, cut the grass, fixed things around the home, cooked, and helped out anytime I asked.

Visualize how great you would feel if your finances were in order, you had a plan to maintain an orderly home, and you had more time for God and your family. Might you feel more compelled to do something God has been leading you to do? Would you feel relaxed while spending time with your family? How might those two forms of order (finances and home) positively affect your relationship with God, your spouse, and your kids? Some of you may have your finances and houses in order, so this may not be an issue for you. Yet, most of us have probably been under an attack by Satan concerning either our finances or a disorganized home life.

Even if you are considered a perfectionist that has spent the majority of your time at home cleaning, you may be neglecting some time with God, your spouse, or children. Spouses are meant to help one another. The world has led us to believe that there are homemaking titles based upon our genders. Well, that's just not exactly true. A husband may be better at fixing things around the home, but he may also have the capability to mop the floors. Just as a wife may be better at cooking, she may also be able to help her husband do some yard work. We need to help one another however we can. This will free up our time to enjoy God and one another. If you are a single parent, you, too, can find a way to free up some time for you. Pray and ask God for help. Maybe there are certain chores that you can ask your children or a family member to assist you in doing. Sometimes we just need to ask for help and learn how to share responsibilities so that we can accomplish more in less time.

Bible/Journal Time

Now, let's talk about studying your Bible and journaling. If you will commit yourself to God, you will start to see positive changes within yourself and your life, so make sure you write about it! You will need to recall those events on days when you need strengthening. You may not journal every day, but you will be blessed by finding the time to study and meditate on God's Word daily. Remember, absorbing scriptures is a powerful way that the Holy Spirit can speak to you. I spent years reading instead of studying the Bible until one of my favorite spiritual teachers, Joyce Meyer, began to explain the importance of really studying God's Word. I recalled the times that I read the Bible just to check it off my list for the day. I was mainly reading it so that I could get God's approval, and I thought that I was doing great, until the Holy Spirit helped me finally realize that God was not impressed by the quantity but the quality. Andre, a friend of mine, had also taught me about the importance of meditating on God's Word. This concept was so new to me, but the message was coming to me in several ways, so I began to try it out.

One day, I had to speak at an event in which I was slightly nervous. I could feel fear starting to rise up in me, but I thought about what Joyce Meyer and my friend Andre said, and I began to draw on this scripture by repeating it over and over in my mind.

> So do not fear, for I am with you; do not be dismayed, for I am your God. I will strengthen you and help you; I will uphold you with my righteous right hand. (Isaiah 41:10 NIV)

All of a sudden, fear left me, and the peace of Jesus rose in me. It was as if a vacuum sucked the anxiety out! That's all it took, and I had a new purpose for reading my

Bible. I began to study the Bible, but I also learned to absorb scriptures that I needed to draw upon to contradict negative things that Satan had been speaking to my mind about myself. I also kept a mental notebook of scriptures that I may need for trials or moments of spiritual attacks. These verses have become my "sword" of the Spirit. I now understand that the authority of God's Word is a sword to the devil.

Just as you need to be fed physically, you need to also be fed spiritually. Feeding your body with physical food helps us sustain our earthly (temporal) life, but filling ourselves with the Word of God helps us stay connected to the Vine and have eternal life.

Prayer/Worship Time

If possible, try to begin and end your day with prayer. With all that is out there, try not to leave your home without praying for God's strength, protection, direction, and intercession in the lives of you and your family for that day! We will discuss the power of prayer in more detail later.

Discipleship Time

In the "You Will Bear Much Fruit" chapter, you will learn the importance of being a disciple and teaching your children to do the same; that is how we bear much fruit. We are called to be disciples! This doesn't mean that you need to run up and down your street shouting, "Clean your house, or you're going to Hell!" Please don't think that statement is true, cause, I would have been there years ago.

Part of being a disciple means that you allow the Holy Spirit to work through you to help others establish their connection to Christ. Hopefully you won't just be a disciple, but you will begin to entice others to become disciples as well. Some of the people that you need to encourage and to be a disciple to are the following:

- Your spouse

- Your children

- Your family

- Your inner circle (people around you the most)

- Your outer circle (strangers that God may direct to you)

Pray for a way to bless others and to strengthen their relationship with the Lord. My conversations were once about my worldly environment or about TV shows (soap operas), but once God started aligning my soul to His will, most of my conversations shifted to Him and building up His kingdom. I rarely talk with anyone without putting God in it! Those conversations are even more entertaining because serving God is fun and rewarding. When led by the Spirit, sharing testimonies (especially supernatural blessings) can be the most exciting moments of your day. You should always set aside discipleship time with your spouse and children. Yet, as the Holy Spirit begins to transform you, you will desire for others to know the power that can live inside them as well!

Time in the Vine

There is no way that you can calculate every moment of your life. Your new schedule will be designed to keep you focused on working together to establish a routine, maintain order, and free up time for God and one another. It is not to confine you to a schedule that keeps you in bondage but should be thought of as a guide to keep you in the right mind-set. I believe that you are about to be blessed by your commitment to an orderly lifestyle and that the Lord will provide guidance from the Holy Spirit as to how to keep your eyes upon Jesus, so that you can bear much fruit!

Note: Jesus represents the Sabbath-Rest, so seek Him, and you will find eternal rest today and every day through your belief in Jesus [based on Hebrews chapter 4]. I pray that you find rest in God and create an orderly routine that produces a holy lifestyle. Only God can give us the type of daily rest that is obtained by believing in Christ, through which we establish a connection to the Vine of Jesus. Through Him, we can form a life that welcomes the Holy Spirit to order our daily steps and relieve us from anxiety!

In their hearts humans plan their course, but the Lord establishes their steps. (Proverbs 16:9 NIV)

Example: Tithing 10 percent time in the Vine	Hours. Minutes
Bible/Journal (36 minutes a day or 18 or so minutes in the morning and evening)	4.12
Prayer/Worship (36 minutes a day or 18 or so minutes in the morning and evening)	4.12
Discipleship (36 minutes a day or more) • spouse • children • family • inner circle (people around you the most) • outer circle (strangers or people in which God may direct to you)	4.12
Attending church (church service and Bible study)	4.12
Total Time in the Vine	16.48 or rounded up to 17 Hours

Time in the Vine	Planned Date of Completion
Step 1: Get your finances in order. (Get replicable financial assistance, and pray for God to open your heart to tithing at least 10 percent of your income to your local church.)	
Step 2: Clean and organize your house (select your deadline 60 days from today).	
Step 3: Use the Schedule Guide to list typical weekly activities.	
Step 4: Pray and seek God for Vine time (journal the changes that you observe).	
Step 5: Complete your Weekly Time-Tracking Schedule (use Schedule Guide for preparation).	
Step 6: Make copies of the Daily Planner, and use it to structure your new daily schedule.	
Step 7: Pray together before you discuss your progress each day with your spouse. Reevaluate your plans after 30 days.	

Time in the Vine	Planned Date of Completion
Step 1: Get your finances in order. (Get replicable financial assistance, and pray for God to open your heart to tithing at least 10 percent of your income to your local church.)	
Step 2: Clean and organize your house (select your deadline 60 days from today).	
Step 3: Use the Schedule Guide to list typical weekly activities.	
Step 4: Pray and seek God for Vine time (journal the changes that you observe).	
Step 5: Complete your Weekly Time-Tracking Schedule. (Use Schedule Guide for preparation.)	
Step 6: Make copies of the Daily Planner, and use it to structure your new daily schedule.	
Step 7: Pray together before you discuss your progress each day with your spouse. Reevaluate your plans after 30 days.	

Use the Schedule Guide to input your current schedule. Pray for your Vine time percentage. Transfer your Schedule Guide information to the appropriate category in your Time-Tracking Schedule, and then proceed to total your time for each category during the week. If married, work with your spouse to uncover ways to help one another alleviate some of your individual responsibilities so that each of you will have more time for God, one another, your children, and discipleship.

Schedule Guide							
	SUN	MON	TUE	WED	THU	FRI	SAT
6:00 AM							
7:00							
8:00							
9:00							
10:00							
11:00							
Noon							
1:00 PM							
2:00							
3:00							
4:00							
5:00							
6:00							
7:00							
8:00							
9:00							
10:00							
11:00							
Midnight							
1:00 AM							
2:00							
3:00							
4:00							
5:00							

Use the Schedule Guide to input your current schedule. Pray for your Vine time percentage. Transfer your Schedule Guide information to the appropriate category in your Time-Tracking Schedule, and then proceed to total your time for each category during the week. If married, work with your spouse to uncover ways to help one another alleviate some of your individual responsibilities so that each of you will have more time for God, one another, your children, and discipleship.

Schedule Guide							
	SUN	MON	TUE	WED	THU	FRI	SAT
6:00 AM							
7:00							
8:00							
9:00							
10:00							
11:00							
Noon							
1:00 PM							
2:00							
3:00							
4:00							
5:00							
6:00							
7:00							
8:00							
9:00							
10:00							
11:00							
Midnight							
1:00 AM							
2:00							
3:00							
4:00							
5:00							

Use the Schedule Guide to input your current schedule. Pray for your Vine time percentage. Transfer your Schedule Guide information to the appropriate category in your Time-Tracking Schedule, and then proceed to total your time for each category during the week. If married, work with your spouse to uncover ways to help one another alleviate some of your individual responsibilities so that each of you will have more time for God, one another, your children, and discipleship.

Schedule Guide							
	SUN	MON	TUE	WED	THU	FRI	SAT
6:00 AM							
7:00							
8:00							
9:00							
10:00							
11:00							
Noon							
1:00 PM							
2:00							
3:00							
4:00							
5:00							
6:00							
7:00							
8:00							
9:00							
10:00							
11:00							
Midnight							
1:00 AM							
2:00							
3:00							
4:00							
5:00							

Please write in pencil so that you can make changes. Use the Weekly Time-Tracking Schedule to input the amount of time needed for each of the categories. Once each category is totaled, your weekly sum should equal 168 hours. Each day changes, so this will be an approximate calculation of your weekly events. Work with your spouse without judging or condemning. This is to make your lives more efficient and to provide order while decreasing your anxiety. This will allow you to determine areas where you may be able to help one another, have more time for God, your spouse, your children, and discipleship. Before you begin, pray for God to guide you during this process and to protect you from the enemy's interference. Ask God to help you design a schedule that is both feasible and productive.

Weekly Time Tracking Schedule			
Time in the Vine	Hours: Minutes	Vital Time	Hours: Minutes
Bible/Journal		Sleep	
Prayer/Worship		Work	
Discipleship		Other:	
Attending Church		Total Vital Time	
Other:			
Other:		Entertainment/Leisure	Hours: Minutes
Total Time in the Vine		Spectator at Sporting Events	
		Recreational Activities	
Body/Mind	Hours: Minutes	TV & Movies	
Eating		Internet	
Exercise		Games	
Learning		Extracurricular Activities	
Grooming		Date Night	
Other:		Family Events	
Other:		Other:	
Total Body/Mind Time		Other:	
		Other:	
Necessary Routines	Hours: Minutes	Other:	
Commuting		Total Entertainment/Leisure Time	
Cooking			
Cleaning		Other Category	Hours: Minutes
Shopping			
Yard Work			
Errands			
Other:			
Other:			
Other:			
Total Necessary Routine Time		Total Category Time	

Please write in pencil so that you can make changes. Use the Weekly Time-Tracking Schedule to input the amount of time needed for each of the categories. Once each category is totaled, your weekly sum should equal 168 hours. Each day changes, so this will be an approximate calculation of your weekly events. Work with your spouse without judging or condemning. This is to make your lives more efficient and to provide order while decreasing your anxiety. This will allow you to determine areas where you may be able to help one another, have more time for God, your spouse, your children, and discipleship. Before you begin, pray for God to guide you during this process and to protect you from the enemy's interference. Ask God to help you design a schedule that is both feasible and productive.

Weekly Time Tracking Schedule			
Time in the Vine	Hours: Minutes	Vital Time	Hours: Minutes
Bible/Journal		Sleep	
Prayer/Worship		Work	
Discipleship		Other:	
Attending Church		Total Vital Time	
Other:			
Other:		Entertainment/Leisure	Hours: Minutes
Total Time in the Vine		Spectator at Sporting Events	
		Recreational Activities	
Body/Mind	Hours: Minutes	TV & Movies	
Eating		Internet	
Exercise		Games	
Learning		Extracurricular Activities	
Grooming		Date Night	
Other:		Family Events	
Other:		Other:	
Total Body/Mind Time		Other:	
		Other:	
Necessary Routines	Hours: Minutes	Other:	
Commuting		Total Entertainment/Leisure Time	
Cooking			
Cleaning		Other Category	Hours: Minutes
Shopping			
Yard Work			
Errands			
Other:			
Other:			
Other:			
Total Necessary Routine Time		Total Category Time	

Make copies of your Daily Planner for your weekly preparations. If married, work with your spouse to plan the following day for each of you. Pray for God to help you structure and organize your day. Ask for guidance and direction. Always pray for your family's protection from Satan and for wisdom to use good judgment. List the time that you plan to wake up first, and then list your following daily plans and the corresponding times for those events. Carry this log with you throughout the day and make adjustments where necessary. Review it with one another prior to the day ending, and discuss areas for improvement. Be understanding, forgiving, and accepting when either of you does not accomplish all that you set out to do in a day. Do not focus on the things that you didn't accomplish. Enjoy your journey and celebrate your positive changes. Thank God for His guidance in helping you establish a life in the Vine!

Daily Planner			
Time	Day:	Planned Events	Actual Events

Make copies of your Daily Planner for your weekly preparations. If married, work with your spouse to plan the following day for each of you. Pray for God to help you structure and organize your day. Ask for guidance and direction. Always pray for your family's protection from Satan and for wisdom to use good judgment. List the time that you plan to wake up first, and then list your following daily plans and the corresponding times for those events. Carry this log with you throughout the day and make adjustments where necessary. Review it with one another prior to the day ending, and discuss areas for improvement. Be understanding, forgiving, and accepting when either of you does not accomplish all that you set out to do in a day. Do not focus on the things that you didn't accomplish. Enjoy your journey and celebrate your positive changes. Thank God for His guidance in helping you establish a life in the Vine!

Daily Planner			
Time	Day:	Planned Events	Actual Events

CHAPTER 4

"If You Remain in Me and I in You"

Part 4: Order in the House!

Summary

Jesus states:

> I AM THE VINE; YOU ARE THE BRANCHES. IF YOU
> REMAIN IN ME AND I IN YOU, YOU WILL BEAR MUCH
> FRUIT; APART FROM ME YOU CAN DO NOTHING.
> (JOHN 15:5 NIV)

- Satan wants your life out of order so that you will feel anxious and unable to fulfill your purposes.

- The more chaotic your environment, the less you may focus on God, your family, your calling, and discipleship.

- God wants us to have order in all aspects of our lives, which include our finances and homes.

- If needed, take a financial course. Pray for God to help you trust Him and begin tithing (10 percent) of your income. Become a responsible steward of God's money, and have faith that He will bless you financially. "Will a mere mortal rob God? Yet you rob me. "But you ask, 'How are we robbing you?' In tithes and offerings. You are under a curse—your whole nation—because you are robbing me. Bring the whole tithe into the storehouse, that there may be food in my house. Test me in this," says the Lord Almighty," and see if I will not throw open the floodgates of heaven and pour out so much blessing that there will not be room enough to store it" (Malachi 3:8–10 NIV).

- Have fun cleaning and organizing your homes within sixty days, and develop a plan to work together to keep it orderly!

- Spouses should work together to establish more free time for God, one another, and their children.

- Establishing a new godly routine and changing the way you may have functioned for years can be planned, purposeful, and calculated, but still led by the Spirit of God.

- Seek God for the percentage of time that you should start devoting to God on a weekly basis. For example, there are 168 hours in a week. So if God lays it upon your heart to devote 10 percent of your time to Him that is 168 X .10 = 16.8. Finish calculating by multiplying .8 X 60 = 48 minutes. Your total Vine Time equals 16 hours and 48 minutes or rounded up to 17 hours a week.

- No one knows you better than the Spirit of God, so you may be led to start devoting 3 percent Vine time to God on a weekly basis. Celebrate whatever time that you feel God lays upon your heart, because God has a plan for your life! He knows what is perfect for your current situation. Do not base your Vine time on anyone else's, and do not condemn anyone for their percentage of time to God. Instead, encourage one another and be joyous about every step taken that moves an individual closer to Christ!

- Time in the Vine includes Bible/Journal, Prayer/Worship, Discipleship, and Attending Church. Your hours in the Vine will be divided by four to consciously fulfill those four categories.

- Begin to absorb the Word of God and rehearse scriptures that pertain to the particular attacks that Satan has been using on you and your family. Allow these scriptures to be your "sword" of the Spirit.

- Ask the Holy Spirit to help you complete the worksheets (Schedule Guide, Weekly Time-Tracking Schedule, and Daily Planner) to guide you toward developing a daily plan that is perfect for you and helps to establish your new exciting life in the Vine!

CHAPTER 4

"If You Remain in Me and I in You"

Part 5: Pray and Seek Guidance

Jesus states:

> I AM THE VINE; YOU ARE THE BRANCHES. IF YOU
> REMAIN IN ME AND I IN YOU, YOU WILL BEAR MUCH
> FRUIT; APART FROM ME YOU CAN DO NOTHING.
> (JOHN 15:5 NIV)

Satan Hates a Godly Plan

Hopefully, your plans are in place or are at least being developed, and you are about to have a financial budget, a clean house, and a new orderly lifestyle! Well, I don't want to burst your bubble, but I wouldn't be your Christian sister if I didn't let you know that Satan will likely begin working overtime to convince you that your plan is impossible for you to carry out. He may whisper to you all types of negative things about how you've never stuck to a plan. There is no telling the tricks that he will pull out of his evil bag. He has stored up information about you and your family in the hopes of deceiving all of you. Refuse to let him win! He has spent too many years attacking your family. It is time for your breakthrough!

I know all this because, one day, I felt an unusually strong attack upon me by Satan. I was working on the book, when all of a sudden, I could almost sense Satan's demonic forces in the spiritual realm doing everything possible to stop me and bring me to my knees. I even felt physically weak and emotionally drained. Normally, I love to talk with God, but during that difficult moment, I almost felt unable to pray; yet I forced myself to reach out to my Father. While on the floor crying to God, I remember searching for a way to speak. I could only question Him about whether He still wanted me to complete the book or whether I was just imagining this whole thing; then, in the midst of my deep wailing, I received a text from a lady at church named Mrs. Brenda. She would have no way (other than the Holy Spirit) of knowing what I was going through in that moment. Her text simply read, "Read Numbers 23:19."

Now, for some reason, the number twenty-three has stood out in my mind since I was a young child. I was always excited if I found myself around anything that had the number twenty-three on it. Suddenly, I was filled with anticipation of what the Holy Spirit was about to say to me. I wiped my tears and began to read the verse in my Bible.

> God is not human, that he should lie, not a human being, that he should change his mind. Does he speak and then not act? Does he promise and not fulfill? (Numbers 23:19 NIV)

It was as if God reached down from heaven and snatched me from Satan's hold! I still want to cry when I think about that moment.

You see, prayers by believers in Christ who are consumed with the Holy Spirit can overcome *all* deceptions created by Satan. So work toward giving God the time that you have agreed to set aside for Him daily, and refuse to allow Satan to have access to your life! I wouldn't be devoting my time to writing all this if I wasn't certain about God's goodness. I believe that God wants me to share my supernatural moments with you so that you will recognize His ability to intercede in your situations and strengthen you too. I could actually write an entire book on the many blessings that I have experienced, but that would only glorify what God has done in my life. I believe that He wants you to have your own biblical journal full of testimonies! I want you to become so consumed by the love of God that you begin to answer God's call upon your life and snatch others away from the grasp of Satan!

When we go through struggles in life, we may not always experience God rescuing us during our exact moment of despair, but we must persevere because there is something great waiting on the other side of our obedience. Remember this verse:

> Consider it pure joy, my brothers and sisters, whenever you face trials of many kinds, because you know that the testing of your faith produces perseverance. Let perseverance finish its work so that you may be mature and complete, not lacking anything. (James 1:2–4 NIV)

There is no greater reward upon this earth than learning to become mature and complete in Christ!

Covenant Deception

I am about to share an analogy so that you will understand how important it is to pray for God's protection over your family. Please understand that if Satan attacks the plans of God, then certainly he will attack our plans, because in all honesty our lives represent the plans of God.

> "For I know the plans I have for you," declares the Lord, "plans to prosper you and not to harm you, plans to give you hope and a future." (Jeremiah 29:11 NIV)

The plans God has for our futures are the real plans that Satan is trying to stop because he hates God's love for us, and he doesn't want any of God's children to have hope or a future. Let's talk about one way Satan is trying to become the enemy of bodily temples and prevent God's plans for His beloved children to be fulfilled.

> Then God said to Noah and to his sons with him: "I now establish my covenant with you and with your descendants after you and with every living creature that was with you—the birds, the livestock and all the wild animals, all those that came out of the ark with you—every living creature on earth. I establish my covenant with you: Never again will all life be destroyed by the waters of a flood; never again will there be a flood to destroy the earth." And God said, "This is the sign of the covenant I am making between me and you and every living creature with you, a covenant for all generations to come: I have set my rainbow in the clouds, and it will be the sign of the covenant between me and the earth." (Genesis 9:8–13 NIV)

The Holy Spirit unveils Satan's deceptions. The devil wants to take that which is beautiful such as the image of the rainbow and the bodies of God's people and corrupt them. The rainbow is about God not destroying earth with a flood. So, Satan tries to take the symbol (rainbow) that God uses to represent the words "not destroy" and use it as a marketing tool "to destroy." The symbol of the covenant rainbow now represents "gay pride" to many who are deceived. Anyone taking part in any sexual act outside of those ordained by a godly union (marriage) between a man and woman are sinning against their own bodies.

Our bodies are the "temples of God," or where the Holy Spirit dwells within the believers.

> Flee from sexual immorality. All other sins a person commits are outside the body, but whoever sins sexually, sins against their own body. Do you not know that your bodies are temples of the Holy Spirit, who is in you, whom you have received from God? You are not your own; you were bought at a price. Therefore honor God with your bodies. (1 Corinthians 6:18–20 NIV)

If this is a sin that is corrupting you or someone that you know, pray often. I'm sure that Satan, being prideful, is proud of the fact that he changed the image of the rainbow within the minds of some of God's children. He wants to destroy anything that glorifies God in this world—especially God's children.

Though gay actually means happy, Satan managed to find a sinful use of the word. The two words *gay* (the homosexual term) and *pride* are abominations to God.

> The Lord detests all the proud of heart. Be sure of this: They will not go unpunished. (Proverbs 16:5 NIV)

> Or do you not know that wrongdoers will not inherit the kingdom of God? Do not be deceived: Neither the sexually immoral nor idolaters nor adulterers nor men who have sex with men nor thieves nor the greedy nor drunkards nor slanderers nor swindlers will inherit the kingdom of God. And that is what some of you were. But you were washed, you were sanctified, you were justified in the name of the Lord Jesus Christ and by the Spirit of our God. (1 Corinthians 6:9–11 NIV)

Become spiritually aware because evil spirits are looming, and they want to devour our families by starting within our minds. As I referenced earlier, sin is sin. Remember even "little white and brown lies" are sin, but the sins that concern me the most are the types of sin that people choose to accept and form a lifestyle around. I am uncovering new sins about myself often; however, when I read the Word or hear a sermon in which the Holy Spirit shows me a new area of my life that is not pleasing to God, I pray and ask Him to change me. It doesn't always happen overnight, but that's why we have the Holy Spirit to guide our steps. I love *all* God's people and pray for them to be filled with the Holy Spirit! I realize that we were all sinners. However, a pure heart and repentance allow those who believe that Jesus is the Son of God and are committed to walking out this life with Him as Lord over their lives will receive the grace to turn from sin. Saint and I have many struggles, but that doesn't stop me from praying for the salvation of God's people when I notice an area in someone's life that needs repairing. Saint and I need and welcome your prayers too.

Though Satan spends a lot of time planning and strategizing to deceive us, I am so thankful to know that we have the power of prayer, faith, the Word, worship, fasting, and speaking in the Spirit to shield and protect us and our children. When we use what God has given us, it gives the Holy Spirit the ability to comfort (counsel, help, advocate, intercede, strengthen, and stand by)!

> He [Jesus] replied, "I saw Satan fall like lightning from heaven. I have given you authority to trample on snakes and scorpions and to overcome all the power of the enemy; nothing will harm you. However, do not rejoice that the spirits submit to you, but rejoice that your names are written in heaven." (Luke 10:18–20 NIV)

Well, we know how to watch for the devil and his demons and how to be on guard, but how do we protect our kids from Satan's schemes? Due to school, social activities, jobs, and sleep, most of us actually have a limited amount of time with our children. How do we protect them from all the worldly influences, especially if they are away from us most of the day?

Faith!

As you know, my life has not consisted of me always being a mature Christian parent. When our son was between the ages of five to eight, we were often called to the school due to an "issue that occurred." I recall when he was six years old, his teacher, Mrs. Harris, had this rule that if students misbehaved, they had to pull a card. These cards were hung in the front of the room. Pulling a card was the first offense and signified a warning. So, one day, while she was teaching, our son got up from his seat and proceeded to the front of the room and pulled a card. Yet, the strange thing was that Mrs. Harris had not asked him to pull a card because he hadn't done anything (*yet*). She was confused and wondered what he was thinking. Well, she was about to receive her answer.

While on his way back to his seat, he stopped at a certain little boy's desk, gave him a hard slap across the face and proceeded to sit down. He stared at Mrs. Harris with a look that obviously meant, "What are you waiting for? You may continue teaching now." He knew what the consequences of his actions would be, so he decided to be proactive and get that pulling the card business out the way before committing the crime.

"Issues that occurred" calls happened frequently. Needless to say, my husband and I, two worldly mind-set Christian parents, had something on our hands. We took our son to church most Sundays, which he hated. We believed in God and taught him right from wrong but were not creating a life in the Vine within our home. My husband and I weren't training him to pray or read the Bible. We would have moments of getting closer to Jesus, then we would get caught up in this world and lose our spiritual focus. One thing we did well was disciplining our son. We stood firmly in our decisions and were a united couple. You would think that with all the firm disciplining and united efforts, things would have improved with him; however, he would accept his punishment and continue his bad behavior.

One day, I was driving down the road and said to God, "I wish I could afford to put my son in private Christian school." The next thought that ran through my mind was so immediate, powerful, and seemed impossible! How could this thought have come to my mind? The bold statement that rose up in my Spirit was, "If all the Christian children were in private Christian schools, who would set the example for the other children?"

That thought didn't even make sense to me because our son was not demonstrating any characteristics of a Christian child let alone any ability to be an example to another child. However, there was a part of me that wanted to believe that it was true. Could my unruly son someday help other children get closer to Christ? I pondered the fact that since there were no visible signs that that question could be related to my son's future, God must had spoken those words to me; therefore, it had to be a prophecy. A *tiny* amount of faith arose in me.

However, years went by, and there were not many signs of positive changes to our son. One day during his fifth-grade year, I was praying deeply because he was battling some issues from a difficult day at school. It was hurting me to watch him suffer so much. I began to pray and cry. I believe the Spirit of God spoke to me just as He did about my grandmother that day by saying, "Your son is going to be fine." I felt at peace and calm, but during that calm feeling came a realization that I only had a limited number of years left to make an impact with him. I could envision him as a spiritually lost man, and then I imagined myself as a grieving mother wanting to turn the clock back and try again. God placed it on my heart that if I wanted to change the path of my son, I had to change the path of myself first. I felt these words deeply. "If I want him to be a man of God, I need to become a woman of God." I made a commitment to change the structure of my life by allowing Jesus to become Lord over my life. I strived to create a life in the Vine around me, and God's extra blessings began to flow from heaven. I still had some strong attachments to the world, but the Holy Spirit was guiding me as to how to release them.

I began to allow daily time for God. During this time, I would pray for my relationship with God to be strengthened and that of my husband and son. I then started praying over my son and with him. I purchased him an age-relevant Bible and assigned reading times. We read at the same pace to help with communication and feedback. We began to pray together nightly and in the mornings, which also strengthened our lines of communication greatly. We also implemented separate prayer time to build our own personal relationship with Jesus. Shortly after putting our new structures into place, God led us to a new church, which became perfect for the whole family. I had no idea how God was about to transform my son's life!

The Hole-E Doughnut

Our prayers for our children are imperative. Our prayers can direct them to the right people, give them powerful words to profess God's goodness, create boldness within them to stand firm for Jesus, and place them right where God wants them to be.

Within months of my decision to change, our son called me to his room and said he wanted to be baptized. I cannot explain the joy that I felt that day. His confession that he wanted to make Jesus Lord over his life would be the most rewarding, impactful, and important choice he would ever make. His life was truly about to begin. My husband was also being impacted by this new life in the Vine within our home. Our environment was peaceful, fun, and loving. So, Saint also started walking closer to Christ.

As our son was slowly being led out of his turbulent phase, he arrived at school early one morning and saw a group of kids holding doughnuts. He loves doughnuts but loves to joke about his dad *really* loving them. He casually walked up to the kids and asked for one of their doughnuts. He quickly realized that this was some type of organized prayer meeting. After he took a bite of the doughnut, a kid began to pray. So he bowed his head, closed his eyes, and jokingly thought about the doughnut he was holding in his mouth and said to himself, *This must be how Dad found Jesus. (Hee-hee! Pray for him.)*

He started attending those First Priority meetings weekly. First Priority is a way for students to share the love and hope of Jesus Christ with other students. God structured a plan that laid a path for our son to become a leader within the group. Following his first presentation to the school, kids walked up to him afterward and said that he changed their lives! More kids started joining the First Priority team. One day in particular, my son gave a powerful message to the kids in which the director of First Priority of North Alabama happened to attend. The kids were cheering and excited; so the following week a dedicated pastor of First Priority, named Pastor Chris, spoke to the children and walked them through the prayer of salvation. Approximately fifty children or more confessed their lives to Christ and walked down from the bleachers to face their peers.

The Spirit of God spoke to me again and stated, "If all the Christian children were in private Christian schools, who would set the example for the other children?"

I was once again amazed by God's power and the way that He prophesized such an amazing moment years prior to its fruition!

Like us, our son has his own battles to fight, but due to the changes we made to incorporate more time for God into our lifestyle, the Spirit of God began to make changes within him. Our son now strives to be a good steward. He encourages kids to go to church, volunteers to help where needed, gives to those in need, purchases Bibles for others, motivates children that are having struggles at home, reads his Bible, and prays; yet, I can still see almost daily how Satan is attempting to lure him away from the Vine. Since we love our children, we must be willing to pray for them every day and develop a good level of communication so that they will be prepared to handle Satan's attacks internally on a daily basis.

In the early part of 2014, Satan was using children to attack our son more. He saw a child take a piece of paper and throw it on the ground. Our son picked it up and told him that was littering. The boy took the paper back, ripped it into pieces, and then proceeded to throw all the tiny pieces to the ground. Our humbled son picked up each one of them and threw them in the trash. He knows that He is a child of the kingdom of heaven, so his role in this life is bigger than that of peer pressure and everyday struggles. God has taught Him that he has a mission and a purpose. He doesn't have time to waste. I can now see how God is working through our son to help change that little boy. God is amazing!

As parents, we have to give in to the authority of our Father, not only for ourselves but for our children, and then the power of God flows, prayers are manifested, faith is strengthened, and lives are transformed. My husband and I were not capable of changing our son. Children need discipline, but all the discipline in the world could not have accomplished what God can do through a little obedience and a *doughnut!*

Prayer and Worship

Personal moments with Jesus through prayer are where love and faith are built. When you consistently combine prayer and worship with the Word of God and journaling, it will become your favorite time of the day. I talk to God and about God all through my day. When led by the Holy Spirit, my testimonies have become one of my forms of worship. They fill my heart with gratitude and also bring others into that same sense of longing for a deeper relationship with our Father as well. I cannot tell you the number of times a day that I have shared a godly story, and the person I was speaking with stated, "That story gave me chills."

As we find our joy in the Lord, life begins to have more meaning because God makes himself visible in many areas of our lives. Joy even rises by being at the right place within the perfect moment to bless someone else. Prayer time is much more than just asking for the things that we desire; it is a time for gratitude and to build a relationship with our Father in Heaven so that we can adequately reach others. Just think about it; we have the ability to talk with the Creator of everything anytime we choose, *and* He provides favor for His children!

So many people are fascinated by celebrities. If you knew that your favorite celebrity was going to call you tomorrow at 7:00 p.m., you would probably be pretty excited! All your friends would gather around the phone with you. This would be a big deal! Is this celebrity able to heal the sick, make the lame walk, or save your child? Probably not.

We have an ability to speak with the Authority over all creation; yet, we sometimes are nonchalant about this relationship. It is a blessing that God even wants to fellowship with us! He cares about what *you* have to say! He is concerned about *your* needs! If that wasn't enough, He has all power to satisfy your needs and the needs of your children!

Teaching our children to value this time with Jesus is so important. Karen Wheaton is a preacher and woman of God who gives me chills when I hear her speak about Jesus. If you are not familiar with her name, then I advise you to research "The Ramp" and the amazing group Chosen. One day, Pastor Karen talked about how she grew up listening to her precious mother praying often. As a young child, she would nestle herself under her mother's arms as she prayed to God. She learned early about the power of prayer and the necessity of it. Our children need to recognize the need for prayer as if it were food. This is an area that I am trying to develop in my children. They may not grasp the love of prayer overnight. However, years of them listening, observing, and experiencing the manifestations of their prayers will awaken them to the fact that they are blessed to have an ability to communicate with the Lord.

Prayer Time with Jesus

Thank God for Loving You and Your Family!

As you pray, thank God for His goodness as you focus upon His power and authority over your life and situation. Pray for direction to help you train your children in the ways of the Lord. Verbalize your transgressions, concerns, and fears. Repent of your sins. Ask Jesus to relieve you of any doubt, worry, or fears. Ask Jesus to build your faith, provide wisdom, knowledge, and insight as to how to be a good parent to each of your children. Ask Him to help you forgive, to let go of past hurt, and to realize your value and worth as a parent. Call upon Him to give you the strength and knowledge to be a spiritual counselor and disciple throughout your days. Request the ability to be able to speak to each child with godly wisdom that is accepted and received deeply within their souls. Request that this wisdom and love for our Father grows within them and is used to magnify the kingdom and glorify our Father. Pray that God protects them from the enemy, shields them from wrongdoings, and aligns them with the favor of God! And most importantly, pray for you and your loved ones to be filled with the Holy Spirit and fully convicted to obey Him! During your prayer time, wait and peacefully listen to what God speaks to your heart. Please learn the prayer that was given to us by Jesus in Matthew 6:9-13.

Prayers and Blessings

I sometimes envision myself approaching the kingdom of heaven, and there's God and Jesus looking at me. I'm all excited and mesmerized by their overwhelming majestic profoundness! Meanwhile, God and Jesus are on the throne, shaking their heads. I'm bowing humbly like, "What's wrong?" Then they state, "You never realized the authority that was given to you upon the earth."

I truly believe that is where so many of us are right now. What would you do differently if you knew that you had the power of Jesus? Would you worry? Think about how differently you would approach this life.

Once you start to realize that by faith your prayers and words have power, you change, and your life changes! This realization makes it undesirable to strictly rely upon your own capabilities. You will begin to question whether you should consult Jesus before selecting toilet paper. Seriously, though, once we rely upon Jesus for most things, the blessings seem to pour from heaven. Our faith pleases God, so He allows kingdom-driven prayers aligned with His will and declared in Jesus's name to be manifested.

In biblical days, fathers didn't just bless their food; they blessed their children! This message is to the spiritual fathers. You still have the power within you! Let your children hear you blessing them. A father's blessings on his children today are just as powerful as when it was done in the days of Jacob (referencing Genesis 27). Both parents should bless their children, but I think it is so important for children to hear their fathers praying over them.

Moms, in the Old Testament, the first powerful woman the Bible speaks about was Deborah. She was chosen to be a leader of the children of Israel because there weren't any men in Israel capable of leading at that particular time. Can you believe that? Not one man … So God gave her the ability to be a powerful leader. So women, if currently you are raising a child without a spiritual husband, God can strengthen you to become an influential woman of God, and, yes, He can give a woman the ability to raise a godly man!

Children are in constant need of prayer and blessings over them spiritually, mentally, physically, socially, financially, and as a motivation to carry out God's will upon their lives. When you pray about your children, seek guidance to uncover their needs, then pray for those needs, and, lastly, have faith and declare that your prayers will be manifested.

The Spirit of God may reveal to you that your child is spiritually wise; yet, he may be shy around others. When you are blessing your child, don't say things such as, "Lord, stop letting him be so shy." This is your time to use your God-given authority to speak His will upon their lives. When you bless this type of child, ask God to help your son or daughter realize that he/she has the spiritual gift of wisdom. Profess that God created him/her with unique characteristics that are needed for the kingdom. Ask God to strengthen their ability to verbalize their thoughts in a way that inspires others to do God's will. Finally, have faith that by asking in the name of Jesus, it will be done. Always remember to speak to your precious children in a way that moves them closer to the kingdom of God.

Prayers for Your Children

Spiritually: Request that your children will have spiritual wisdom and that God will strengthen them with the fruit of the Spirit (referencing Galatians 5:22–23) and gifts of the Spirit (referencing 1 Corinthians 12:7–11). May they learn to listen to the Holy Spirit and develop a heart to study the Word, worship, pray, and align their souls to God's will.

Mentally: Ask the Lord to guard and protect their thoughts and actions, and give them wisdom to do well in school. Pray for them to not be led by their emotions but by the desires of their Father in Heaven. May they guard their tongues and profess what is righteous.

Physically: Seek the ability to teach them to be healthy and strong. Ask for protection over their bodies and the ability to make wise decisions concerning their flesh. May the desires of the flesh never supersede the desires of the Lord.

Socially: Pray for the Lord to guide their steps when choosing friends. Request that their experiences will bring joy to their lives. Call upon the Lord to teach them to be a blessing to others. May they learn to search the heart of man instead of the outer appearance of man.

Financially: Ask for financial favor and the desire for them to give to every good work. May they always tithe, provide for their families, and earnestly seek ways to bless others.

Motivation: Ask the Lord to give them the yearning and faith to carry out God's plan for their lives. May they strive to walk in the ways of the Lord and learn to hear and adhere to the voice of God.

Thank the Lord for blessing you and your family!

Praying in the Spirit

Now as you know, there was a lot of shouting and arms flapping in that old country church that I grew up in, but you would not find the members speaking in tongues there! I believed that speaking in tongues was weird, and people stopped doing that once the Bible was completed. If you were like me, you may not even have known that speaking in tongues was one of the spiritual gifts from God. I wonder how people were led to believe that once the New Testament was over, some of the spiritual gifts of God just seemed to vanish. Hmmm, do you think someone we know was responsible for that deception?

> All of them were filled with the Holy Spirit and began to speak in other tongues as the Spirit enabled them. (Acts 2:4 NIV)

One day, a lady at our new church named Mrs. Leslie gave me a book about speaking in tongues. Now I already had a relationship with God, and I was experiencing miracles in my life. God was also providing me with prophetic wisdom, and the Holy Spirit was guiding me in many areas of my life. So when she gave me a book about speaking in tongues, I felt as though it was completely unnecessary. I also thought to myself, *Uh-oh! She is one of those people!* I thought I had concluded why the Bible tells us that Christians are peculiar people.

Though this idea was completely against my teachings, I had developed a level of respect for this lady, so I was enticed to understand how such a remarkable woman of God could still believe in speaking in tongues. So I began to read the book.

Hmmmmm. By the way, I wonder how many of you have non-Christian friends that might want to know more about God if you gave them a book like the Bible.

Okay, so back to the speaking in tongues book.

The book gave instructions on how to speak in tongues, which made me feel even weirder. It stated things like once you feel the Spirit upon your body, begin to make vowel sounds. I'm thinking, *If it is from God, shouldn't you just automatically start speaking in tongues? Why is there an instruction booklet as to how to do it?* The book stated that sometimes it does happen naturally, but many people have to be "trained" to do it.

The word *train* must be so vital to our connection in the Vine.

The book talked about how if we never opened our mouths or never learned to speak in our regular language, how would we be able to communicate with Jesus? It was a compelling viewpoint, so I continued to read the little booklet quickly. After reading it, I was rather intrigued. No one was home. So I went to my prayer place in the house and began to make sounds like the book directed. I waited for God to do something, but I just felt like a babbling baby. I thought God must be laughing at me. I then began to pray in English.

Sometimes I can feel the Spirit upon me in prayer when my right hand starts to quiver. Once that occurred, I started babbling again like the book directed, just to try it out once more. Finally, just as the Spirit took over my right hand, it took over my tongue. And there came my new spiritual language with God. I didn't know what I was saying, but I knew that I didn't have control over my tongue anymore. It had to be the Spirit of God. I was amazed, but I thought that I couldn't tell anyone about this. I asked God to reveal to me what I said. The book said sometimes God will reveal it to you right away, but sometimes it may be in a conversation. Well, I believe God revealed it to me later that day and left me saying, "Wow, God!" In English.

That same day, I had lunch with a friend. I often prayed privately for this friend to forgive others. I wanted to tell her about my new language, but I thought, *No way; she will think I'm crazy!* Anyway, while at lunch she began to tell me about how that morning out of nowhere she realized she needed to forgive her husband. She said she felt as though she needed to look internally and to realize that she's not perfect either. I nodded, as I ate my lunch, and was so happy about her new spiritual awakening. She proceeded to talk about how we have all made mistakes and should be forgiving. Now, I don't ever remember her talking about opening her heart to forgiveness before, but I am not making a connection between this story and my new language.

Until …

She then stated that she came to the realization about all of that that morning, and it felt like I was somehow involved in her new level of forgiveness! That sent me into my "Wow, God!" moment. So I asked the next logical question, "Around what time did you have this new revelation?" She said, "I don't know, but it was this morning probably around nine or nine thirty." I began to scream in this country little restaurant. I yelled, "Around nine-ish this morning, I started speaking in tongues!"

Well, no more hiding it from the world now.

> In the same way, the Spirit helps us in our weakness. We do not know what we ought to pray for, but the Spirit himself intercedes for us through wordless groans. And he who searches our hearts knows the mind of the Spirit, because the Spirit intercedes for God's people in accordance with the will of God. (Romans 8:26–27 NIV)

Remember earlier when I talked about our son developing a closer relationship with Jesus through the doughnut? Well, the Spirit of God knows things about him that I do not. It is impossible for me to know everything or to chase him down at school and say, "Don't hang around with that child! Don't play that game on that child's phone! Don't view those naked pictures!" However, the Holy Spirit can do all that and so much more. The Spirit can lead him to walk toward a doughnut instead of toward a child that is trying to entice him to make a wrong decision. The Spirit of God can speak to him and let him know how to respond to a certain situation. The Spirit of God can also give him courage and boldness to speak about Jesus. I honestly believe that I was led to the speaking in tongues book to equip me with the spiritual gift of knowledge to write this book.

So let me just say, if you were like me and against speaking in the Spirit, I would advise you to read about it. There are many books out there on the subject, but be careful about what you choose. It should always align with the Bible. I don't remember the name of the book the lady gave me to read, because I returned it to her to pass along for someone else's use once I completed it. However, our church family read the book called *The Holy Spirit*, by John Bevere, in which John did a great job explaining more about the Holy Spirit and His role in our lives.

Ask God to help you incorporate speaking in tongues in your daily spiritual structure and get ready for your lives to be impacted!

Jesus said:

> "If you love me, keep my commands. And I will ask the Father, and He will give you another advocate to help you and be with you forever—the Spirit of truth. The world cannot accept him, because it neither sees Him nor knows him. But you know Him, for He lives with you and will be in you." (John 14:15–17 NIV)

The Bible gives instructions about speaking in tongues. Make sure you read (1 Corinthians 14). We are to use our gifts but as a means to edify individuals and glorify our Father in Heaven.

Praying and Fasting

> Jesus answered, "It is written: Man shall not live on bread alone, but on every word that comes from the mouth of God." (Matthew 4:4 NIV)

In 2015, our pastor asked us to begin fasting and join the pastors in prayer every Wednesday. Once I began doing it, God began to shift my thoughts. Fasting is not a diet; however, I am going to share a message about how fasting affected my diet. In the past, I overate a lot. I tried all types of diets. I often lost weight and then regained it all back. I seemed to have minimal control over my eating or my mental thoughts surrounding eating until I made a consistent choice to fast once a week.

One day, while I had overeaten, I felt sluggish and didn't want to talk to anyone. People were trying to contact me for counseling, but I was unable to think clearly to help them. I prayed and asked God to help me. And in that moment, He finally delivered me from over thirty years of suffering. I felt these words, "When you are overeating, you cannot answer my call upon your life." Then God placed a desire in me to eat food as close to the way that He provided for us as possible.

All of a sudden, I became appreciative of all the natural food that He had given us. Fasting became a way to break my flesh and allowed me to clearly receive a message from God that may have likely saved my life. Fasting is humbling and allows us the ability to focus upon the Lord. It allows the Spirit to rise in us. We need to be reminded that we are the house of the Spirit of God. We are sacred temples; therefore, we should be able to allow God to have control over our bodies and not allow our temples to be ruled by any fleshly desires.

The Bible didn't speak about fasting as something you can do if you would like. It is something that we are expected to incorporate into part of our spiritual structure, and it is for our benefit!

Jesus] said,

> "When you fast, do not look somber as the hypocrites do, for they disfigure their faces to show others they are fasting. Truly I tell you the truth, they have received their reward in full. But when you fast, put oil on your head and wash your face, so that it will not be obvious to others that you are fasting, but only to your Father, who is unseen; and your Father, who sees what is done in secret, will reward you." (Matthew 6:16-18 NIV)

As you can see, Jesus kept saying *when* you fast, not *if* you fast. However, many people are on so many medications and have many health issues today. So talk to your "structured Christian" doctor and pray for guidance to find the best method and time frame for you to use when fasting and praying.

Be Thankful

Try to begin and end each day in worship by aligning your heart with thoughts of the many blessings that our Father, Jehovah-Raah (the Lord my Shepherd), has provided to you and your family. When we are grateful to God, it fills our hearts with love for Him. Aren't you thankful that God has given us all the steps we need to make it through this life and to train our children to do the same? We have the Word to study daily so that it will become like flesh to our bodies, or what I like to call our internal textbook. It builds our faith and gives us direction. Our prayers and worship time are a way for us to communicate with Him about our gratitude, needs, wants, and concerns within our hearts. Then, we have a special language through the Spirit that communicates with the Lord on our behalf making known what is needed to stay on the spiritual path and help others. The Spirit of God inside us also sends messages through thoughts, visions, dreams, conversations, books, and many other ways to guide our steps and help us to parent effectively.

The Holy Spirit comforts and provides a peace that goes beyond any earthly understanding. We have a way to humble ourselves before our Lord, saying we will temporarily abstain from physical sustenance, so we can build our spiritual relationship with our Father! Do these things so that you will see the supernatural power of God manifest, thereby transforming your life and the lives of your children. If all these things weren't already enough, God also gives us individual talents, spiritual gifts, and an ability to live by the fruit of the Spirit so that we may bear much fruit!

CHAPTER 4

"If You Remain in Me and I in You"

Part 5: Pray and Seek Guidance
Summary

Jesus states:

> I AM THE VINE; YOU ARE THE BRANCHES. IF YOU
> REMAIN IN ME AND I IN YOU, YOU WILL BEAR MUCH
> FRUIT; APART FROM ME YOU CAN DO NOTHING.
> (JOHN 15:5 NIV)

- Satan wants to sabotage God's plan for you. So don't be deceived by any thoughts, situations, or circumstances attempting to undermine the process that your family has set in place to move closer to Christ.

- Let God build your faith through perseverance. Be joyous over your situations by knowing that staying connected to Christ means that you are victorious!

- As you uncover sin in yourself and others, pray for a conviction by the Holy Spirit to make the necessary changes in your lives. Always forgive yourself and your loved ones when the changes are not occurring as quickly as you may have envisioned because the process may be part of the victory.

- In God's timing, your prayers and faith can unleash a supernatural intercession in any situation, so never stop the clock with God.

- Be thankful that we can talk to God anytime! Have a grateful heart and remember to worship the Lord daily.

- Pray for your children daily and bless them by professing goodness over their lives. Use the power of the Holy Spirit in you to lead them closer to the kingdom of Heaven.

- Pray for your children spiritually, mentally, physically, socially, financially, and to be motivated to carry out God's will upon their lives.

- Be thankful for all the ways that you can defeat the devil and remain in the Vine of Jesus: the Word, prayers, worship, fasting, speaking in tongues, and the Holy Spirit!

CHAPTER 5

"You Will Bear Much Fruit"

Part 1: Love God, Love Others, Be Disciples

Jesus states:

> I AM THE VINE; YOU ARE THE BRANCHES. IF YOU REMAIN IN ME AND I IN YOU, YOU WILL BEAR MUCH FRUIT; APART FROM ME YOU CAN DO NOTHING. (JOHN 15:5 NIV)

Gifts from Heaven

Bearing much fruit is our task in this world. God made us to be fruitful. He created us to produce. When He converts our temporal minds to His eternal way of thinking, we realize that we have an important task of building up God's kingdom by leading our children and many others to Christ. Lately, I have seen several "feel good" type of videos being shared online, such as people buying groceries for people, building homes for the homeless, and demonstrating forgiveness to those who hate. There is a warm and fuzzy feeling deep down inside us when we see or experience moments like those. I believe the Spirit of God uses those things to create joy inside us. Many people in the world today are sad and depressed because they have not used their lives for the correct purpose of helping others, so their joy lies vacated, waiting to be filled. God made us in His image; therefore, the things that will ultimately bring us happiness must also bring Him happiness.

Spiritual gifts are given to us as we mature in Christ, but the fruit of the Spirit grows within us as God sends revelation to us through scriptures, trials, and spending time with God. The fruit of the Spirit is how we demonstrate that we belong to Christ to others. It is what leads others to Jesus. When the spiritual body grows in both the spiritual gifts and the fruit of the Spirit, life is transformed. When our children are born, we must create a life in the Vine that demonstrates the fruit of the Spirit: love, joy, peace, patience, kindness, goodness, faithfulness, gentleness, and self-control. As they grow in Christ, God will provide spiritual gifts such as: wisdom, knowledge, faith, healing, miraculous powers, prophecy, the ability to discern between spirits, speaking in tongues, and the interpretation of tongues. He also strengthens their ability to live by the fruit of the Spirit, which energizes them to fulfill their purposes.

Fruit of the Spirit and Spiritual Gifts

(Galatians 5:22-23, referencing, and 1 Corinthians 12:7-10)

Fruit of the Spirit	Spiritual Gifts
Love	Wisdom
Joy	Knowledge
Peace	Faith
Patience	Healing
Kindness	Miraculous Powers
Goodness	Prophecy
Faithfulness	Distinguishing between spirits
Gentleness	Speaking in different tongues
Self-control	Interpretation of tongues

Three Purposes of Our Lives

As soon as your children have understanding, it is time to teach them about their three purposes in life that Jesus commanded of God's people.

(Matthew 22: 37–40 and Matthew 28:18–20, referencing)

Three Purposes of Our Lives
Love the Lord our God with all our hearts and with all our souls and with all our minds
Love others as we love ourselves
Be disciples (Help others have a relationship with our Lord) and (make disciples)

The sooner your children realize their three purposes, the easier it will be for them to make the right choices in life. We know we should love the Lord, and most of you by now probably believe in helping others get closer to Christ. However, some of you may be thinking, *How is it possible in this day and age for us to teach our children to love others as they love themselves?* Well, first of all, let me state, this is not possible without the Spirit of God. When we encounter people who are lost spiritually or need help, something should begin to rise in us that causes us to help. Many in this world are corrupt, cunning, and ruthless, so there's a generation of young people that believe success in life is accomplished by possessing narcissistic traits. This belief is completely incongruent to God's Word.

Here is a little insight into my previous character: I was extremely competitive to the point that I had to consciously suppress it at times. Everyone who truly knew me was aware of it. Finally, one day, I could feel that the Lord wanted me to do more to help those around me succeed. I kept thinking, *If I help others, they may outperform me.* Yet, the feeling that I should help those around me succeed was so intense that I started helping others regardless of my concern for my own success. It opened a floodgate of blessings! God started rewarding me and them simultaneously. He's God, so He has enough blessings for us all. I then felt joy like never before. God was teaching me to love others and to delight in the success of others as well as myself.

Can you imagine the difference in the world if we all adhered to our three purposes? Well, the world is waiting on our children to be a part of the change. You don't have to teach your children the ways of this world in order for them to prosper because God will provide for those that love Him.

Following Jesus

Simon Peter and some others went to catch fish one night. Simon Peter's fishing expertise probably made it known to him that fishing at that particular time and location was a wise decision. However, this particular night they didn't catch any fish. Early the next morning, Jesus appeared. He told them where to cast their net. The Bible says their net was then full of (153) fish. Allow Jesus to tell you how, when, and where to cast your nets, and blessings will just appear.

(Referencing John 21)

Talents

Many of us grew up hearing the story (referencing Matthew 25:14-30) about the master with the talents (money in this case), who gave a portion of his talents to his servants since he was going away on a journey. To one he gave five talents, to another two, and to another one. The man who received five invested them and made five more; the one who received two invested them and made two more. The master was proud of those servants and rewarded them; however, the one who received one talent just buried it and then returned that same talent right back to his master. The master was outraged at this servant because he was lazy and had not been profitable with what had been entrusted to him. He took away the talent from that man and demanded that he be thrown into darkness, where there will be weeping and gnashing of teeth.

I often think about this when I look at all the people in the world who have received special talents (our creative abilities) and gifts from God; yet, many people bury their talents or keep them hidden. Some use them for their own profitability. Others use them for sinful or evil purposes. I do not want any of us or our children to misuse the talents that God has entrusted to us.

Children are blessed with physical or mental talents that can be used for them to benefit the kingdom and for them to prosper upon this earth in a way that would be pleasing to our Father. For instance, if you have a daughter who loves to cook, you may be thinking that she could one day own a restaurant and create a successful business. However, when your soul is being aligned to think like God, you may pray about ways to use her talent for discipleship. You might be led to have her bake treats while she's young to take to nursing homes and other facilities. Maybe she could personalize cookies with crosses enclosed in decorative bags attached to notes that have uplifting Bible verses to drop off at someone's home. Always pray with your children to create ways to use their talents to demonstrate love, bring joy, and provide a spiritual awakening to others.

If that little girl is taught to think like God throughout life, she may grow up to own a nonalcoholic Christian restaurant. Can't you see the Bible verse engraved napkins on the tables? Visualize an enclosed play area for the kids to enjoy biblically related toys and books. Do you see the stationed areas with large-screen TVs broadcasting contemporary Christian music videos? Occasionally, a local Christian band could provide entertainment. Extra tip box locations are strictly used to pay for a family's meal of the day. Waiters are trained to pray with people when their food arrives at the table.

Hey, by now you should have gotten accustomed to my unique way of thinking.

Seriously though, can you imagine the possibilities of how this one restaurant could affect change upon a city? Some non-Christians would have to stop by to witness what it was like inside. Perhaps a nonbeliever might be walking through a difficult time and is led to stop by this restaurant. I can see people being converted the moment the waiter begins to pray for them. There's no limits to the things our God can do when we seek Him for guidance!

I know that is my imagination running rapid, but I seriously wish the Spirit would lead some of your older kids to create that restaurant for my family!

Even at the thought of all those positive things, Satan likely began to whisper to some of you, "A nonalcoholic restaurant won't be in business long because that's where they make the most profit." Well, that's what Satan wants us to think; nevertheless, if God directs its creation and timing, it will be blessed.

Seriously, have you ever looked at the lines at Chick-fil-A? That's not happenchance …

You may be saying, "My son or daughter is good at a sport, math, or likes to plant flowers, but how can that be used toward the kingdom?" I certainly don't know! But, you know who does!

Whatever your child's talent may be, pray with your children, acknowledging their talents, and give thanks for their abilities. Then ask God for ways to uncover how their talents can be beneficial to His kingdom. An important factor to remember is that just because your child is good at something may not mean that his or her talent is a lifelong goal. Always train your children to let God lead them. That talent is for a reason; it may or may not be their destiny; yet, seek God as to how it can still be a blessing.

When this purposeful life is developed early, children can even begin to occupy their minds and time with searching for ways they can bless others. I believe that many kids and adults have become unfulfilled because they are missing the fulfillment that comes from being disciples. Our son spent too many unproductive years playing video games, so we are still trying to release him from that grasp. It's great to have fun playing, but we must monitor the things in our lives that are attempting to occupy most of our thoughts and time. Real joy comes from things that reach our hearts.

Bringing It All Together

(Fruit of the Spirit and Spiritual Gifts + Talents = 3 Purposes)

Three Purposes of our Lives
Love the Lord our God with all our hearts and with all our souls and with all our minds
Love others as we love ourselves
Be disciples (help others have a relationship with our Lord) and (make disciples)

Fruit of the Spirit	Spiritual Gifts
Love	Wisdom
Joy	Knowledge
Peace	Faith
Patience	Healing
Kindness	Miraculous powers
Goodness	Prophecy
Faithfulness	Distinguishing between spirits
Gentleness	Speaking in different tongues
Self-control	Interpretation of tongues

The moment our children have understanding, it is our job to provide structures and to begin the process of sharing the knowledge of our Creator. The purpose is for you to use your talents as a model for them during the very early stages of your children's lives. For instance, if God has given you a creative talent, you might be led to use your toddler's painted hands as an imprint on a canvas, and then you might inscribe a Bible verse within their little painted handprints. God may give you the wisdom (spiritual gift) for you to let your toddler present this gift to someone at a hospital or to an elderly neighbor.

Write a short story in your toddler's journal about this experience and date it or draw a picture describing this day, letting your little one color it. Read this story from his or her journal at bedtime, explaining how God loves everyone and how the two of you were a blessing to someone that day. Labeling the picture with the fruit of the Spirit that matches the journal entry is a great way for children to learn about how to treat others very early in life. Your toddler will grow to understand that his or her talent + fruit of the Spirit + gift of the Spirit = three purposes. In this example, the parent used his or her gift of wisdom to allow the talent combined with love (fruit of the Spirit) to accomplish these three purposes: love God, love others, and be disciples.

I believe that even at birth, our love for others flows into their little hearts. I remember when my son was a baby. God had placed it on my heart to give to this certain homeless man often. I began to see that man so often that it was as if he had a schedule for my random daily events. (Note, at that time, and in the area we are from, it was rare to see the same homeless man.) Now let me remind you, Saint and I did not have much money at all! Saint had a job that he dressed up for in the daytime, and then he worked at a grocery store at night just for us to make ends meet. Yet, there I was running through the park during the day giving all my available cash to a homeless stranger.

When God was first leading me to do this, I felt so embarrassed and nervous; yet, it never stopped me from running to give this poor old man money. It didn't matter how bad the weather was; I would often park my car somewhere and run to chase this man down while carrying my son. I am not advocating doing this, but I felt convicted by the Holy Spirit to do this. I now know that God had a lesson for me.

After many weeks of seeing that man, one day it felt like God spoke to me and said, "You will go back to college and graduate with honors." God gave me faith that what He told me was true. Right after I signed up for college, I saw that old homeless man in the library reading. We made eye contact with each other and smiled. I never saw him again, but that moment felt as if God had placed him there to silently confirm, "You are on the right path."

Now, our son is extremely giving. He saves and gives, but rarely spends money on himself. If he sees a child at school not eating lunch, he would rather give the child his lunch than to just watch him or her not eat. I thought, *Where did that come from, God?* Then, I remembered me running with him to help that old homeless man and all the other times he saw us giving. Saint and I were not living perfect lives, but that form of obedience to God was still forming a special spiritual gift in our son. As God is training our son to give, He is also blessing him. We are astonished by all that God is demonstrating to him. That is what's so great about the Holy Spirit; as parents, we only have to instill the training, but then God takes over and provides the supernatural!

As your children grow, they will develop their own talents and later gifts of the Spirit that can be shared with the world through discipleship. Pray for outreach ministry opportunities and make those times fun for your kids. Call their friends over to help, or make it a special parent/child moment. Once this lesson is taught at an early age, children build a confidence in their abilities to become disciples. They learn to discuss Jesus more easily with people and to share His love for them. They develop a love for others and have a greater sense of purpose for their lives.

The chart below provides a visual flow of what has been discussed in this chapter. It's so important for your children to know their purposes, to focus upon God, and to combine the fruit of the Spirit, spiritual gifts, and their talents in order to promote discipleship and grow God's kingdom.

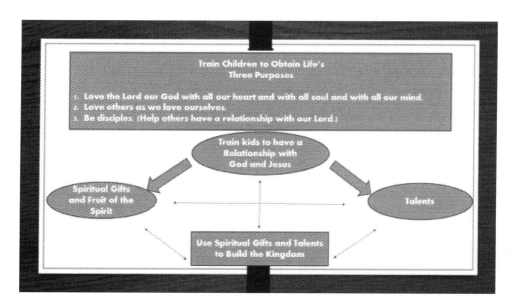

The Pit or the Fruit

I hope you now have a better understanding of why so many young adults feel so empty or lost. As humans, we were not created simply to enjoy the tangible things of this life. We are spiritual beings, and, until we learn that, it is impossible to find satisfaction strictly within things of the world. I hope that one of the first things you learned in life was the word *love*. You probably didn't understand its meaning at first, but you felt it because love is spiritual. Training your children for their greater purposes equips them to understand God's love for them and to return that love to God and others. This love allows them to handle life's difficulties and motivates them to make the right choices. When you are filled with this love for Christ, it is noticeable through the fruit of the Spirit and may cause other people to become curious about the key to your happiness.

As our children grow and develop, so should our parenting style. This will be discussed in the next chapter, but we should think of stages of parenthood in phases that consist of ages zero through six, seven through eleven, twelve through eighteen, and nineteen and older (or the young adulthood stage). I pray that there will be a generational awakening where parents will begin to train their children in the ways of the Lord at birth. However, if you were like my husband and me, you may have been a little late to the ark. Many children raised in Christian homes never learn the rewards of a life in the Vine. By now, you know that that term represents a life filled with a love for Christ and exemplified by the fruit of the Spirit. Parents must learn to demonstrate the excitement of living a life in the Vine. It's remarkable to watch the transformation in kids when we make our life in the Vine joyous and exciting!

Let's think about what our children are up against! There are Satan and his crew, which we will call "the Pit." They are working overtime to paint this picture of how great it is to be on their team. The Pit have these wickedly enticing shows, thrilling movies consisting of violence and sexually alluring content, sensory heightened video games, immorally appealing books or magazines, booming songs filled with vulgarity, sinfully interactive stimulating technological devices, sensory overloading drugs, and a host of friends willing to pull them deeper into the pit. Whew! However, our children generally don't see those negative innuendos. Like many adults, they are blinded by the pleasure. Unfortunately, even if they are aware of the wickedness, without the proper training, the temptation may supersede the negativity.

All of that is what Satan wants to pull our Christian kids toward. The Pit may seem to be it! And here we are talking about Jesus and church. We want them to take one or two days a week and get dressed up in stuffy clothes to sit and be quiet while a boring person talks, yells, or teaches stories about dead people. I know that sounds harsh, but sometimes that's how they see some churches.

Not our church by the way. It is awesome! Pastors Rusty and Leisa, we absolutely love you and all our anointed pastors! And hopefully you attend an awesome church too!

In addition to going to church, we also want our children to read their Bibles, pray, and then be good little boys and girls while they watch the Pit crew appear to have so much fun. It's easy to understand why so many children stray from a life in the Vine. Some Christian parents have stated life is not supposed to be about fun and enjoyment because it is about doing the will of our Father in Heaven.

Well, it really is about doing the will of our Father. However, I don't believe that God would give us the ability to laugh unless He wanted us to laugh. I believe He wants us to have fun! In your homes, one of the main steps to training your children to be godly children is creating a life in the Vine. Brand your home as the "atmosphere of God!" Let it be joyous. Incorporate the fruit of the Spirit. Get rid of the Pit and fill your home with the fruit (love, joy, peace, patience, kindness, goodness, faithfulness, gentleness, and self-control.) Your ability to create the atmosphere that matches the fruit of the Spirit will bring forth much fruit!

The use of your kids' talents in addition to their spiritual gifts and fruit of the Spirit that our Father in Heaven has given them promotes self-confidence, value, purpose, and a spiritual awakening that their lives are more important than a self-driven highly sensory intoxicating moment that comes with detrimental consequences. For instance, if you have a son that loves video games and is very creative, instead of buying him the most violent, action-packed, adventurous games, pray about the situation. Maybe you will be led to other games that are fun and that promote intellectual growth without violence or sexual content but provide the inspiration to stimulate his creativity. Seek God because you may be raising a son that will develop exciting video games that highlight the stories of Moses, Gideon, or David.

Honestly, I don't see how anything can be more exciting than some of those stories in the Bible!

Think about ways to reduce a few of the Pit crew members. Why does the Pit have so many cool-looking things going on over there? It's often because Christian parents have not done a good job discovering their children's talents, focusing upon their three purposes, or praying that their children determine the ways they can provide benefits to our society's spiritual development. Our children should have the opportunities to play games, watch movies, read fun books, hang out with friends, and create enticing environments that are greatly appealing to the Pit crew. Imagine if some of the smartest business entrepreneurs of our time were trained to focus on their three purposes. Can you imagine how those same gifted minds could have played a major role in our Christian lives and in kingdom growth?

It is our job as parents to monitor where we spend our money. There's no need to invest in things that create more Pit crew members, and especially not to allow those things into our homes for entertainment of our Christian children. One day, after I had taken inventory of my kids' things around the home, whether given or purchased ourselves, I realized we no longer had to ask why godly children strayed, because part of the answers were right in front of us. Once we became spiritually aware, we found ways to create the fun without including the sinful things.

I am so thankful that the Holy Spirit has given me discernment about this now. I can almost look at a sassy preteen girl and determine the type of shows she or her friends are watching due to their behaviors. Many teen shows appear harmless because they carry the logo of a so-called kid-friendly business that we have grown to trust. Yet, if you sit down and watch some of those shows, you will start to see many attitudes and behavioral traits that you would not like your child to present to the world. However, if this is part of our youths' entertainment, it often becomes part of their character. So, parents, please pray for discernment, wisdom, and solutions.

God can give us clarity about our lifestyles, our atmosphere, our children's gifts and talents. Request from God ways in which you can train your children to develop their particular talents for the kingdom and in some cases for their financial prosperity. Enhancing those talents will create the life in the Vine that is perfect for them. It will bring meaning to their lives. They will start to learn early the rewards of being a Christ follower, and they won't try to fill those missing gaps by being a part of the Pit. Don't conform to the world. Entice the world to conform to God. The world needs our children!

Journal Moment (Love Promotes Discipleship)

List the three purposes that Jesus commanded of us and the fruit of the Spirit. Begin to teach them to your children. Prayerfully, seek in your heart to discover which of the fruit of the Spirit needs to be strengthened within your home. Write about your commitment to begin your personal journey of creating an "atmosphere of God" within your home. Remember, always start with yourself first; and, through prayer and faith, trust God to bring along the rest of your family. List some of your talents and those of your children. Now pray for ways to use these talents for discipleship.

Write down the ideas that come to you.

Have fun experiencing your new life in the Vine!

Share your inspirational stories with other parents!

CHAPTER 5

"You Will Bear Much Fruit"

Part 1: Love God, Love Others, Be Disciples
Summary

Jesus states:

> I AM THE VINE; YOU ARE THE BRANCHES. IF YOU REMAIN IN ME AND I IN YOU, YOU WILL BEAR MUCH FRUIT; APART FROM ME YOU CAN DO NOTHING. (JOHN 15:5 NIV)

- We are called to bear much fruit, or in other words to lead our children and *many* others to Christ.

- We experience real fulfillment and joy in life when we learn how to be a blessing to others.

- The fruit of the Spirit (love, joy, peace, patience, kindness, goodness, faithfulness, gentleness, and self-control) is how we demonstrate that we belong to Christ. Seeing these traits in us is what leads others to the Lord.

- As our connection to Christ grows, God can give us spiritual gifts such as: wisdom, knowledge, faith, healing, miraculous powers, prophecy, the ability to discern between spirits, speaking in tongues, and the interpretation of tongues.

- We have three purposes in life: love God, love others, and be/make disciples. The sooner our children are convicted to live by their three purposes, the easier it will be for them to make the right choices in life.

- God gives us individual talents and abilities that should also be used to glorify the kingdom of God.

- When you notice a talent in yourself or your children, seek God as to how it can be used for His purpose.

- When we combine the fruit of the Spirit, spiritual gifts, and talents to fulfill God's purpose, we are living by our three purposes (love God, love others, and be disciples). For instance, if we love God, then it is demonstrated by the fruit of the Spirit (the way we live and treat others). God gives us spiritual gifts (such as wisdom and knowledge), which will inform us as to how to use our talents and abilities to be His disciples and build up God's kingdom.

- Have fun training your children to think like God, not like the world, and, as they grow, they can become fruit producers and snatch people from the Pit.

CHAPTER 5

"You Will Bear Much Fruit"

Part 2: Parenting Stages

Jesus states:

> I AM THE VINE; YOU ARE THE BRANCHES. IF YOU
> REMAIN IN ME AND I IN YOU, YOU WILL BEAR MUCH
> FRUIT; APART FROM ME YOU CAN DO NOTHING.
> (JOHN 15:5 NIV)

Building a Strong House Called "the Temples of God"

A parent's love for Jesus is the key factor to raising a godly child! Once your heart and mind is focused upon pleasing our Father in Heaven, then you can fully begin the process of training your children to make Jesus Lord over their lives too. The Spirit of God will shield your hearts and minds from attacks of the enemy. You will delight in your life in the Vine and begin to seek ways to be disciples and to create disciples.

Though parents may love the Lord, it can be difficult to realize that their parenting skills must grow and develop along with the growth of their children. The techniques used to train a child that is six years of age requires alternative methods by the time that child approaches age thirteen. Please look over the table below to familiarize yourself with the four stages of parenthood that will be discussed throughout this chapter. These stages are strictly based upon your child's introduction to Christ. During the discussions of this topic, there will be moments when correcting behavioral issues need to be discussed. However, the purpose of these stages is to train a child in the ways of the Lord.

Keep in mind that selecting your beginning stage will be based on the "Parenting Levels" instead of the "Ages." The only exception to this is if your child is a young adult. Think of the "Parenting Levels" as your process of forming a sturdy home. The formation of a home begins with the "Foundation." God is the True Builder and Jesus is the overseer. Parents should learn how to joyfully become servants of God, which can lead their children to desire to be the house or dwelling place of the Spirit of our Lord.

> For every house is built by someone, but God is the builder of everything. "Moses was faithful as a servant in all God's house," bearing witness to what would be spoken by God in the future. But Christ is faithful as the

Son over God's house. And we are his house, if indeed we hold firmly to
our confidence and the hope in which we glory. (Hebrews 3:4–6 NIV)

I pray that your lives are structured in such a way that you are now ready to be a servant
of the Lord and for God to be able to work through you to build those strong houses
(your children) centered on Christ! In the analogy throughout the "Four Stages of
Parenthood," parents will be referenced as the builders, though we know that nothing
godly can be built without God. The term *builders* in these analogies refers to parents
working as the servants of God.

Four Stages of Parenthood		
Stages	**Parenting Levels**	**Ages**
Stage 4	**Advising or Friendship (Roof)**	**Ages 19 and Up (Adulthood)**
Stage 3	**Coaching (Bricks)**	**Ages 12–18**
Stage 2	**Teaching (Walls)**	**Ages 7–11**
Stage 1	**Disciplining (Foundation)**	**Ages 0–6**

Those of you reading this book will be starting at different stages of parenthood because
your kids are of different ages, have diverse experiences, and have various starting points
in reference to their relationships with the Lord. Some of you may have middle-school-
aged children and are just now starting to introduce them to building a relationship
with Jesus, or you may be a parent of a toddler. Whatever your situation, we need to tie
it all together and put everyone on the same page.

These stages are categorized by ages and parenting levels. So if your child is of a certain
age, yet you haven't had the opportunity to focus upon the information in the preceding
parenting level, then, you need to begin at the parenting level that best describes your
situation. Meaning, if you have a child whose age is within the range of 7–11, which is stage
2, yet, you never built the foundation for your child, then you will need to start at stage 1.
Please allow the Spirit of God to guide you toward the process of advancing to stage 2. Look
over the chart and determine your beginning stage by the information within the parenting
levels. Since the ages of each stage have a range of years, you should have time to train your
children in the ways of the preceding stages and then gradually advance upward toward
their accurate age category. The goal is to allow the Spirit of God to work through your life
and to keep you at a pace that is appropriate for your family's growth and development.

If your son or daughter's age is within the range of stage 4 (adulthood), then you may not be
able to revisit the preceding stages. However, if you are just starting within this age group,
you still have an ability for your child to be a godly man or woman. However, you will rely
more on God's intercession, and we all know that He is more than capable to change any
situation. Suggestions will be discussed later as to how to be an advising parent and still

direct your children toward God during this stage. The closer your relationship is with your child, the easier it will be for you to still make an impact. Nevertheless, adults of all ages are still answering the call of Jesus, so keep praying for your children. Prayers work!

The earlier you begin this process, the longer you can sow seeds into your children. Your years with your children will pass extremely quickly! If you don't believe it, you must be raising a toddler. Those years seem to take forever while you are living through them. Yet, if you ask any parents that have a child who just graduated from high school, those parents are often trying to revisit past memories when their children were younger. Though they may be proud of their accomplishments, many parents are still left wondering if they prepared their children enough for the world.

So, think about your kids' ages at this moment. Think about the opportunities that lie ahead. Visualize the type of man or woman that you want them to become. How do you want them to handle problems? What type of marriage would you like for them to have? How might you want them to parent your grandchildren? And, most importantly, are you training them in the ways of the Lord, so that their names will be written in the kingdom of Heaven? As I previously stated, I believe that God has placed this book in your hands for a reason. He wants you to start making some changes so that you won't look back and regret not taking the time to lead your children to the most valuable gift that Jesus offered at the cross—The gift of life!

You are about to learn four stages of parenthood that will enhance
your ability to lead your children closer to Jesus!

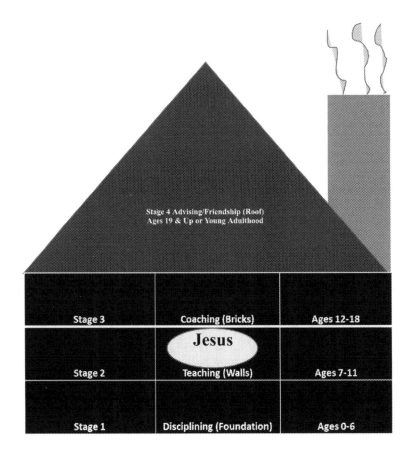

Stage 4 Advising/Friendship (Roof)
Ages 19 & Up or Young Adulthood

| Stage 3 | Coaching (Bricks) | Ages 12-18 |

Jesus

| Stage 2 | Teaching (Walls) | Ages 7-11 |

| Stage 1 | Disciplining (Foundation) | Ages 0-6 |

Now I'm no architect, but thankfully my Father is the greatest of architects!

Stages of Parenthood

Stage 1 or the Disciplining Level (Foundation)

Everyone knows that a house is not assembled by first creating the roof. It must be constructed from the bottom to the top. Raising godly children is like building a strong house. If you want your structure to stand firmly, then it needs a solid foundation. The purpose of the foundation is for that formation to be the first stage of development. This is stage 1 or the Disciplining Level. The foundation sets the standard as to the sturdiness of the home.

Stage 2 or the Teaching Level (Walls)

Now it's time to add the walls. If the foundation is in place properly, it can be good support for the walls. This is stage 2 or the Teaching Level. The walls define the meaning of the foundation. If assembled properly, the walls will be built around the Chief Cornerstone (Jesus) who will protect the dwelling.

Stage 3 or the Coaching Level (Bricks)

Stage 3 is the Coaching Level. This is when the bricks will be added to provide stability. The bricks will likely receive some damage from a few strong winds. Therefore, the builders (parents) may need to make some adjustments, so that the house is formed to withstand some powerful storms ahead.

Stage 4 or the Advising/Friendship Level (Roof)

Last is stage 4, which is the Advising Level. The roof will be added, establishing its completeness. Gradually, the builders (parents), will begin to walk away. The builders will check on the home and will never fully abandon its creation. Though the home will likely need some repairs here and there, if Jesus, the Chief Cornerstone, has found His dwelling inside the home, it will last forever (eternity)!

May the Spirit of the Lord Live Inside Your Children

For, he himself is our peace, who has made the two groups one and has destroyed the barrier, the dividing wall of hostility, by setting aside in his flesh the law with its commands and regulations. His purpose was to create in himself one new humanity out of the two, thus making peace, and in this one body to reconcile both of them to God through the cross, by which he put to death their hostility. He came and preached peace to you who were far away and peace to those who were near. For through Him we both have access to the Father by one Spirit.

Consequently, you are no longer foreigners and strangers, but fellow citizens with God's people and also members of his household, built on the foundation of the apostles and prophets, with Christ Jesus himself as the chief cornerstone. In him the whole building is joined together and rises to become a holy temple in the Lord. And in him you too are being built together to become a dwelling in which God lives by his Spirit. (Ephesians, 2:14–22 NIV)

The Building Permit

Parents need to understand their roles as builders and begin to function by the approval of the Lord. There is a very important relationship that parents must understand. Spiritual marriages are sacred to the Lord. Your homes will be blessed because you love God and seek His righteousness. However, the alignment of your home is key to your happiness and to the way God ordained the family structure. The husband and wife must become one. This union must function with Jesus as the center of your heart and as the head of the family. The Holy Spirit must dwell among the united parents, forming one union, led by one Spirit. This is a powerful formation. Children are part of this family unit but do not take precedence over the united husband and wife, and definitely not over the head of the household, God.

Spiritual husbands were created to be the leaders of the family; though, they are of one body with their spiritual wives. Man was created to lead by receiving direction from God and adhering to His Word. Both parents' role is to model the behavior of Christ so that children will know how to love and live like Jesus. A mother should also be led by the Spirit of God and is expected to provide help and support to her husband in a loving and respectful manner. Both parents should be humble and exemplify the fruit of the Spirit by striving to create an "atmosphere of God" around them at all times. Spouses should always remember that this godly union is a symbol of His love.

When both parents model Christ's behaviors and move through the parenting stages of disciplining, teaching, coaching, and advising, a sturdy home will be built. Please note, children will change and develop automatically. They will likely grow toward Christ or away from Christ. That's why this process is all about the parents learning to create positive changes within their children and instilling a desire for them to move toward Christ.

Regardless of the stage of development you are currently implementing, the preceding chart demonstrates the flow of parenting godly children. The only areas of the chart that will change are the parenting stages and the process in which you approach their growth. You will use this graph as a guide for all stages. The basic premise is to model the behavior that Christ expects from us, by fulfilling our three purposes and by being led by God, Jesus, and the Holy Spirit. Husbands and wives should strive to spiritually become one, train children according to their stage of development to ensure they make good choices, enhance their experiences, help them form positive relationships, and promote discipleship. Dads and moms should be functioning as one entity.

However, it is a dad's responsibility to train a son to someday become a husband/father, and it is a mom's responsibility to train her daughter to someday become a wife/mother. Always model the behavior that God wants them to model when starting their families and raising your future grandchildren.

If you are a single parent, you have a direct line to God, and He can give you all that you need to ensure that your child becomes a man or woman of God! Base your decisions on the will of your Father in Heaven. Allow the Spirit of God to direct you, and you too will be amazed by God's plans for your life.

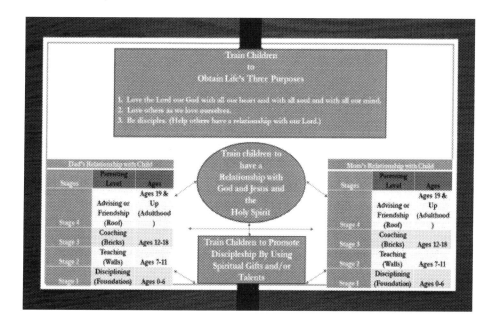

When All Odds Seem to Be Against You

You may have a spouse who doesn't have a close relationship with Christ. Please understand that it is God's design that a father and mother become unified and teach their children to fulfill His purposes. Nevertheless, the first thing a godly parent must realize is that he/she cannot control his/her spouse's relationship with God. The best way to encourage someone to desire a life of Christ is to pray for them, and then "you" must always strive to exemplify the characteristics of Christ. Remember that you are not alone. God cares about your concerns, and He has plans for your life. Oftentimes, there are hurtful situations from the past that at least one parent may mentally bring into the household. Parents may also have previous childhood experiences that have led them to select inappropriate parenting styles. If you are in an unsafe environment for you or your children, *please* seek help, and remove yourself and your children from an environment that is harmful or detrimental.

Some parents share a difference in beliefs, which may lead to various disagreements. This often places the family unit out of proper alignment with God. Blended families are also becoming a new form of reality, which may mean more people, more ideas, and fewer godly principles being demonstrated in front of your children. You could probably list a page full of differences among you and the individual or individuals that are involved in the parenting of your kids. Those circumstances may cause you to feel frustrated and hopeless at times. Always remember that God loves you and your child. He wants his/her future to be good! You may feel like there are too many negative conditions against your choice to raise a godly child, but never give up on God's ability and willingness to intercede in any situation that is incongruous to His Word! I have personally seen God step into situations and turn things around. The only way it could have been more visible that it was Him would have been for the clouds to open so we could watch all His magnificence descend from heaven. Though we didn't visually see that happen, it was still such a spiritual intercession that we knew it was our Father's supernatural powers at work!

You have an Almighty force in agreement with your choice to train your child to remain in the Vine of Jesus! So whatever your current family status may be, by having faith, focusing on your relationship with the Lord, living a life in the Vine, and praying, God can allow your children's lives to become spiritually prosperous. The way to properly train a child is by *you* building a personal relationship with Christ and following the Word of God. Adhere to God's alignment and lovingly provide disciplining, teaching, coaching, and advising, so that your children will forever desire to be led by the Spirit of God.

Please, remember to start with the appropriate parenting Level instead of the ages. However, if your child is approaching adulthood, you will begin at stage 4. Make sure you read each of the parenting stages because God will likely provide you with wisdom that you will find useful for any of the other stages.

Let's go!

CHAPTER 5

"You Will Bear Much Fruit"

Part 2: Parenting Stages
Summary

Jesus states:

> I AM THE VINE; YOU ARE THE BRANCHES. IF YOU
> REMAIN IN ME AND I IN YOU, YOU WILL BEAR MUCH
> FRUIT; APART FROM ME YOU CAN DO NOTHING.
> (JOHN 15:5 NIV)

- A parent's love for Jesus is the key factor to raising godly children.

- Our parenting skills must grow and develop along with the growth and development of our children.

- This book was designed to first align parents' hearts to Jesus so that they can help build the love of Christ in their children.

- Raising godly children is like building a strong house; the parents are the builders, and Jesus is the Chief Cornerstone.

- The four parenting stages are: stage 1 or Disciplining Level (Foundation), stage 2 or Teaching Level (Walls), stage 3 or Coaching Level (Bricks), and stage 4 or Advising/Friendship Level (Roof).

- The best way to lead others to Christ is for *you* to exemplify the characteristics of Christ inside and outside of your home.

- It is very important for each parent to focus upon his or her personal relationship with Christ and pray for his or her spouse and children.

- Pray for your family unit to be structured so that it is in proper alignment with God's plan. (God is the head of the entire family; next is the godly husband, and then the godly wife, and lastly are the godly children.) If you are a single parent, you have a direct line to Jesus, and He can equip you with the wisdom needed to raise your children.

- Keep striving to be more like Christ daily because God will be on your side. No matter the negative circumstances surrounding believers, the Holy Spirit is within them; and there is no force more powerful than God!

CHAPTER 5

"You Will Bear Much Fruit"

Part 3: Stage 1 or Disciplining Level (Foundation)

Jesus states:

> I AM THE VINE; YOU ARE THE BRANCHES. IF YOU REMAIN IN ME AND I IN YOU, YOU WILL BEAR MUCH FRUIT; APART FROM ME YOU CAN DO NOTHING. (JOHN 15:5 NIV)

Three Purposes of Our Lives
Love the Lord our God with all our hearts and with all our souls and with all our minds (wise choices)
Love others as we love ourselves. (Build solid relationships and form good experiences)
Be disciples (Help others have a relationship with our Lord) and (make disciples)

As you advance through each of the parenting stages, set the three purposes of our lives as your main parental training goal. Watching the manifestation of these purposes within the lives of your children will give you such joy, especially when the desire to fulfill their purposes is etched in their hearts forever!

Stage: 1	Parenting Level: Disciplining (Foundation)	Ages: 0–6
Everyone knows that a house is not assembled by first creating the roof. It must be constructed from the bottom to the top. Raising godly children is like building a strong house. If you want your structure to stand firmly, then it needs a solid foundation. The purpose of the foundation is for its formation to be the first stage of development. This is stage 1 or the Disciplining Level. The foundation sets the standard as to the sturdiness of the home.		

Disciplining often has a negative connotation to it. However, it should be thought of as a way for our children to learn structure, guidance, organization, and the proper way to behave. Disciplining our children doesn't end at age six, but children between the ages of zero to six need a strong amount of disciplining in place. This is also your most opportune time to sow the love of Christ into their hearts. Think about how much your children learn during the first phase of their lives. It is remarkable! Their brains are equipped with billions of neurons ready to work. It is the best time to begin establishing your children's fun life in the Vine and training them to move toward their purposes.

You are about to guide your kids toward their prosperous futures! However, if you are raising some really little ones right now, you may be experiencing some temper tantrums, sleepless nights, and have a desire to hide for a moment just to have some peace and quiet. This is often a very difficult stage of parenthood; yet, it really is over before you know it!

Hee-hee, I know you don't believe me.

Hang in there because if my husband and I survived, God can bring you through it too. The odd thing is that once our children grow we have a hard time remembering things from their earlier years. It's hard to grasp, but our babies really are only babies for a year. Twelve little months out of their entire life is all the time you will have to just love, rock, and hold them.

Thankfully, if you are raising a child within stage 1, there is no one that should be able to have a greater influence on their lives than you and/or your spouse. What you sow should be predominately what they are valuing. Sure, there will be outer influences attempting to affect them, but never in their lives will you have as much authority to affect their beliefs as you do at this moment. You are about to show the world what God can do through you to bring up a child! By modifying the behavior that God would like for them to portray to the world, you can build the foundation that seals their three purposes into their hearts and minds. You can build such a remarkable legacy and truly begin to teach others what it means to be fruitful!

Communication

One of the first things parents may need to modify is the way they communicate with their children. Their little baby ears probably began listening to the cute, sweet tones of their parents. Yet, when those babies transitioned into rambunctious youngsters, over the years, their parents' voices may have evolved into forceful, pounding, repetitive noises. At least that's what happened in our household. Instead of yelling, teach your youngsters to obey your commands the first time by speaking kindly but firmly. Make direct eye contact to capture their attention and train them to obey you without your voice reaching octaves made for the ears of dogs.

Teach them about respect, by using words and phrases that move them toward the kingdom of God. I have often heard parents (especially us) yell to their children, "Bring me this, or bring me that!" It is our job to train our children to form good relationships in life. Forming good relationships is a way to bring them closer to the kingdom. If a child yells to another person, "Bring me that!" "That" statement will probably not form a good relationship with the other person. Learning proper communication is one of the greatest ways to move your child closer to the kingdom of God.

Our son wanted me to let you all know that his mother still hasn't mastered the proper communication of tone … That child!

Remember, this age group loves to model the behavior of their parents. That is why it is so important for us to be aware of the way we speak to them, to others, and about others. Your tongue can be one of the most dangerous parts of your body, so please learn how to use it effectively for the kingdom of God.

> Likewise, the tongue is a small part of the body, but it makes great boasts. Consider what a great forest is set on fire by a small spark. The tongue also is a fire, a world of evil among the parts of the body. It corrupts the whole body, sets the whole course of one's life on fire, and is itself set on fire by hell. (James 3:5–6 NIV)

Journal Moment

Believe me, maintaining proper communication with your children is not always easy. However, if this has been an issue for you, start making changes today by imagining that your interactions with your children and communications around them would be videoed and shown at church next Sunday. Mm-hmm, gotcha! Pray for God to reveal the areas of communication that need altering.

Enjoy writing about your changes and experiences in your journal.

During this stage, it may sometimes be cute to hear your child begin to use phrases as an adult. Due to the behavior he or she may have observed from adults, your child might begin to demand many things in forceful tones, or he or she may model some negative adult mannerisms. Sometimes, adult traits noticed early in children are entertaining. We may even view their behavior as a sign of intelligence. Parents may be led to believe that they will correct the behavior once their child is older. This could not be further from the truth. Any behavior that you would not want your child to exemplify in the future needs to be corrected the moment it is observed. Sometimes, you may have to walk away to chuckle first, but return quickly for the moment of correction.

I have heard parents say that their child is demanding because he or she is a leader. If they are meant to be leaders, God will certainly arrange for it to happen. Their calling will not be changed by a little godly disciplining. Our motto is, "Don't raise the bar!" Think of the bar as their bad behavioral traits. When you allow a negative behavior to escalate (example, eye rolling, aggressive behavior, rudeness, selfishness, sassiness, talking back, lack of gratitude, not responding to you the first time, lying, misbehaving, etc.) you are allowing the bar to be raised. It's not easy to lower a bar that has been raised, especially as our children get older. You may not notice the bad behavioral trait reversing immediately, but if you continue to stand your ground, over time you should not be dealing with some of the same issues. It took years for us to see an improvement in our son, but my husband was consistently correcting bad behaviors. When God began to take control over our son's heart, all the years of disciplining correlated with God's Word, and he began to change. God has great plans for your children, so pray and ask Him to give you the grace to keep that bar low!

Please remember that important tip.

Let's bring an awareness to this topic by revisiting the home that we are constructing. You have just laid the foundation; however, you notice that it isn't level. Instead of repairing it, you proceed to add the walls (stage 2); yet, due to the faultiness of the foundation, assembling the rest of the structure would cause it to become unstable. You think to yourself, *If a storm comes, the house will collapse easily.* It is now a lot harder to work backward to fix the damage that could have been corrected before the walls were added (stage 1).

Disciplining During Stage 1

Let's discuss the type of disciplining that we do not like to consider. Parents often have various opinions about how to handle improper conduct. When possible, disciplining should be administered after prayer. By the time your child starts understanding, it's time to start teaching the word *no*. In our home, we have two very different children. As you know, our son was a turbulent little boy during this stage. By the time he was clearly aware of his actions, he started receiving a spanking when he purposefully did something that he knew that he shouldn't have done. We had to teach him that there were consequences to his negative choices in life. On the other hand, our daughter has managed to avoid spankings. Disciplining her mainly requires a motivational speech.

Our son wishes he had been trained by her when he was younger.

I must say, Saint is one of the best disciplinarians I have ever seen. I wish he would teach a course to parents about disciplining children. He catches many things that I miss. He demands respect, but his love for them is still present. He doesn't allow the children to manipulate us in order to get what they desire. All I can say is that I am often amazed at his ability to create order in our home when it comes to our children. Believe me, when we were raising our son during this stage, that was not an easy task.

As you move closer to Christ, the Holy Spirit can even guide the process of disciplining your child. God appreciates the fact that we are attempting to raise children to live righteously. A child should never be abused in any way! Whenever possible, it is beneficial to pray and calm down before disciplining. This will allow you to let God direct you. Yes, we even need God to direct us when we are talking to our children concerning their bad behaviors. Then, strive to discuss the situation that led to the punishment with your child and explain the proper way for them to behave in the future. Be forgiving, and explain in an age-appropriate manner why their behavior was unacceptable and why you chose the disciplining that you selected. Move them closer to Jesus by recognizing their good behavioral traits and referencing characteristics of Christ that you see in them.

When our daughter was four, we discovered that she lied about pulling some fancy material off my decorative pillows. Now, there were three things she loved right under God: her family, dessert, and her *stuffies*. Due to the fact that she lied, her dad took all of her stuffed animals away from her. She was devastated! That night, she asked for God's forgiveness and also said, "God, please help me to get out of this mess and get a stuffy back." Whew! That was so sad to watch because she was so hurt and remorseful about lying. Though she was young, we had to be firm and immediately begin the process of putting an end to lying.

Before proceeding with the touching ending to this story, you need to know that she had a favorite joke, which she would often tell family members and friends. It went like this:

Her: "Where did the cows go on their first date?"

Us: "Where?"

Her: "To the moo-vies!"

Okay, now back to the story. You will see why that *hilarious* joke was important soon.

Due to the fact that she didn't have any stuffies, she cried herself to sleep that night. The next day, we were scheduled to do missionary work at a place that we had never visited. She was still very sad the next morning but remained helpful getting things ready for the mission work. She pushed the carts of dessert to the car and helped get things in order. Along with the church, we delivered socks and dessert to a home for disabled veterans and the elderly. She began to sing "Twinkle, Twinkle Little Star," which caught the attention of a man who called himself Walt Baby Love. He sang her favorite song, "Amazing Grace." Then he said, "I will be right back." He came back with a brand new stuffy. It was a *cow* stuffy. He then said, "I was led to give you this."

She looked up to God, smiled, and said, "Thank you, Jesus." She had tears in her eyes but began to tell Walt Baby Love her cow joke. She knew that God had just answered her prayer. That was her favorite joke, and out of all her stuffies that her dad had taken away, none of them were cows.

She then said, "My dad took all my stuffies because I didn't tell the truth."

He said, "Your dad is not going to take this one." Walt Baby Love remained a friend and later joined our church after that event! That day became a symbol in her journal titled "God's love, faith, and forgiveness."

Later, she received all her stuffies back and introduced them to "Moo Moo" the newest member of the stuffy family. After that event, lying was rarely an issue with her. If she caught herself attempting to lie, she felt convicted to apologize and immediately tell the truth.

God had a special surprise for us during that teaching moment. He actually turned that true story into a published book. You can find it online or at many of your local bookstores. It's called *The Day I Met Walt* by Aleesa St. Julian. By age six, our daughter became a published author and began reading her godly book to hundreds of kids. Her testimony has been shared through many avenues including television. Sadly, Walt died six months after the release of her book, but we were blessed to have several years to enjoy him in our lives. Before we met him, he was homeless for about thirteen years of his life. Yet, weeks before his death, he professed that he was ready to be with Jesus because he had a good life, and now he was leaving a legacy behind.

This was the last scripture that he read to me days before he passed away:

> And I thank Christ Jesus our Lord, who hath enabled me, for that he counted me faithful, putting me into the ministry. (1 Timothy 1:12 KJV)

From left: mom (Mary), son (Avery), hubby (Saint), daughter (Aleesa), myself (Terita), and friend/family (Walt Baby Love)

Photograph was taken the day Aleesa launched her book. She served the community with the Huntsville Dream Center, church members, family, friends, teachers, and loving people all throughout the city. Five months after this photo was taken, Walt went to be with his heavenly Father on his seventieth birthday.

You see, we are going to have moments that our children need to be disciplined. However, God can take our trials and even our past sins and turn them into our most miraculous testimonies. God wants to be included in all areas of our lives. He wants you to recognize His involvement in your child's upbringing. So pray for wisdom and guidance for each particular child. Tell God that you desire to have faith in His ability to help you properly raise your children, and then journal about your remarkable events.

The most amazing part thus far of *The Day I Met Walt* is the fact that children are taking that little book to their schools and using it for show and tell. They are also reading it to their friends. God will reach His people, and you may be amazed at how He plans to use you and your children to do it!

Stage 1: Building a Godly Foundation

The table below is a summary of how combining the specific structures, fruit, talents, and gifts will lead them toward reaching their purposes upon this earth. *Structures* consist of the particular actions we take to hold ourselves accountable and grow closer to Jesus. As a parent, we must make a choice to implement the structures. Regardless of feelings within a given day, we must train our children to devote their time to Jesus. The *fruit* will be the same for every age category. This may be the hardest age to notice the fruit of the Spirit in your children, but don't give up. Through prayer, they will start to grow within them. As for *talents*, children are all so different. The table obtains examples of attributes or abilities that you may observe in your children early; however, your child will exemplify his/her unique talents as he or she grows. Remember to pray about his or her specific talents and discuss it with him or her; then, ask for ways to use it for the kingdom. It may be just for the purpose of a smile, but if an elderly person doesn't have any grandchildren visiting her, that smile may do wonders to her spirit. The *gifts* of the Spirit may start to surface once your little ones begin to accept Christ into their hearts. The *purposes* column is our ultimate goal for ourselves and our children. Use this table as a guide toward building a foundation for your youngsters, and have fun!

Ages 0–6 Years (Disciplining)				
Structures + Fruit + Talents + Gifts = 3 Purposes				
Structures	Fruit	Examples of Talents and Attributes	Gifts	Purposes
Weekly church service	Love	Artistic	Faith	Love the Lord our God with all our hearts and with all our souls and with all our minds!
Daily children's Bible stories	Joy	Leader	Wisdom	Love others as we love ourselves!
Daily worship music and praise time	Peace	Sociably appealing	Knowledge	Be disciples (help others have a relationship with our Lord)!
Daily prayer time	Patience	Witty or entertaining	Healing	
Tithing and giving	Kindness	Energetic	Miraculous powers	
Picture journaling	Goodness	Athletic	Prophecy	
Make Jesus fun!	Faithfulness	Helpful	Distinguishing between spirits	
Talk about God, Jesus, and the Holy Spirit many times daily!	Gentleness	Encouraging	Speaking in tongues	
Share stories to build faith	Self-control	Strong-willed	Distinguishing between different tongues	

Use this table to fill in the talents and any gifts of the Spirit that you may notice in your stage 1 children. If you have more than two stage 1 children, make copies of this chart. Write your child's name on the front. Remember to pray for God to reveal ways in which your family's life may bless others. Record your experiences in your journals.

Ages 0–6 Years (Disciplining)				
Structures + Fruit + Talents + Gifts = 3 Purposes				
Structures	Fruit	Examples of Talents and Attributes	Gifts	Purposes
Weekly church service	Love			Love the Lord our God with all our hearts and with all our souls and with all our minds!
Daily children's Bible stories	Joy			Love others as we love ourselves!
Daily worship music and praise time	Peace			Be disciples (help others have a relationship with our Lord)!
Daily prayer time	Patience			
Tithing and giving	Kindness			
Picture journaling	Goodness			
Make Jesus fun!	Faithfulness			
Talk about God, Jesus, and the Holy Spirit many times daily!	Gentleness			
Share stories to build faith	Self-control			

Use this table to fill in the talents and any gifts of the Spirit that you may notice in your stage 1 children. If you have more than two stage 1 children, make copies of this chart. Write your child's name on the front. Remember to pray for God to reveal ways in which your family's life may bless others. Record your experiences in your journals!

Ages 0–6 Years (Disciplining)				
Structures + Fruit + Talents + Gifts = 3 Purposes				
Structures	Fruit	Examples of Talents and Attributes	Gifts	Purposes
Weekly church service	Love			Love the Lord our God with all our hearts and with all our souls and with all our minds!
Daily children's Bible stories	Joy			Love others as we love ourselves!
Daily worship music and praise time	Peace			Be disciples (help others have a relationship with our Lord)!
Daily prayer time	Patience			
Tithing and giving	Kindness			
Picture journaling	Goodness			
Make Jesus fun!	Faithfulness			
Talk about God, Jesus, and the Holy Spirit many times daily!	Gentleness			
Share stories to build faith	Self-control			

Forming a Solid Foundation

Ages: 0–6

- Purchase a large booklet with blank pages or with a few added lines as their journal.

- Disciplining: form structure, create a godly environment, provide age-appropriate consequences for actions, set expectations and stick with them (don't raise the bar).

- Teach them their three purposes in life.

- Demonstrate and teach them the fruit of the Spirit.

- Pray for God to uncover their talents, to strengthen the fruit of the Spirit, and to develop in them spiritual gifts. Pray for guidance as to how their particular attributes or talents can be used for the kingdom of God.

Between the ages of zero and six years is the best time to provide structure and discipline. Try to attend church regularly. Help your little ones find friends who have "structured Christian parents." Every day should include a Bible story, prayer time, and worship music. Formulating a standard time for each brings excitement and makes learning about Jesus a rewarding experience to young children. Build an excitement around Jesus! Say things such as, "In thirty minutes we are going to worship Jesus!" In their journals, draw pictures to represent how God's goodness is visible in their lives. Create fun ways to help them remember scriptures that will allow them to understand God's love and power. In some cases you can label the pictures using the fruit of the Spirit that matches the images. As they grow, let them help you color and draw in their journals, and remember to date each entry.

In upcoming years, their journals will help them retain things that God has done in their lives. It will also help to establish faith. Even sad days can be an entry into their journals along with prayer requests. Make sure to reference and date prayers that were answered by God. Teach them to pray for themselves and others.

This is also a great time to worship with them through Bible study time and through spiritual music. Thank Jesus often in their presence. Try to refrain from complaining about your days because you want them to learn how to be thankful. By doing this, they will learn to be aware of their blessings daily. Teach them to take money to church weekly to promote tithing. Explain how though it may be a small amount of money, when all the children of the church put their money together, it can provide a lot of help to those in need. At our church, the younger children chant, "I love to give to God!"

Glorify God in all things, from a walk in the park, to a trip to the grocery store. Discuss some of the great things God is doing in your lives right now. Tell them you love them but always let them know that God and Jesus love us all more than we can even imagine! Stretch your arms to demonstrate the height or depth of God's love for all of us. Let them hear you thank God for giving them to you. Tell them your stories that glorify Jesus or demonstrates the ways God has built your faith. When having imaginary play, create your own fairy tale stories that promote kindness and goodness (fruit of the Spirit).

Demonstrate faith in God instead of fear of the unknown. Don't wait for the death of a loved one to discuss heaven. By talking about how wonderful heaven will be and how great it will be to someday see God and Jesus, you may prevent them from blaming God when they lose someone close to them. Explain how God calls us to heaven in His time. Make sure they know the story of Jesus and why it is so important for them to make it known to others. Teach them to be missionaries from birth by encouraging them to help others by being generous or sharing their toys. When these acts of kindness are noticed, relate them to the fruit of the Spirit. Discuss how happy it makes Jesus when they care for others. When you notice something they like to do, or something that comes easily for them, pray for ways to teach them to use it to benefit the kingdom.

Again, this is not an easy age to manage. Parents are often bombarded with overwhelming feelings that life will never be peaceful again. However, remain faithful that God has a plan for your children. If you invest the time to pour the love of God into their hearts early and maintain it throughout their years with you, you will reap the rewards of your marvelous labor. If you work diligently to build this foundation from birth and throughout stage 1, it will be easier to maintain it and harder for the enemy to demolish it. With your focus upon the Lord, Jesus will become their chief cornerstone. Satan is still looming, but he's no match for God! Despite what you may see, believe that their bodies will become the holy temple of the Spirit of God! Your role is to train your children to make God part of their daily lifestyle and to fully rely upon Him. God will provide the favor, blessings, and supernatural moments!

CHAPTER 5

"You Will Bear Much Fruit"

Part 3: Stage 1 or Disciplining Level (Foundation)
Summary

Jesus states:

> I AM THE VINE; YOU ARE THE BRANCHES. IF YOU
> REMAIN IN ME AND I IN YOU, YOU WILL BEAR MUCH
> FRUIT; APART FROM ME YOU CAN DO NOTHING.
> (JOHN 15:5 NIV)

- Stage 1 or the Disciplining Level is the time for parents to build a godly foundation in the lives of their little children.

- As your children age, reevaluate the foundation that you have been building and ask yourself if you are *daily* sowing a knowledge and a love for Jesus in their little hearts before you progress to stage 2.

- Your children learn an entire language during stage 1, so this is the most opportune time to train them about the love of God.

- During stage 1, you have the most influence in their lives, so begin to train them to align their souls with the will of God. Teach them how to care for others, understand God's love, and desire to do His will instead of following the path of the world. This will help prepare them for stage 2 (a time when outer influences of the world become more prevalent).

- Please guard your tongue, watch your temperament, and respect your children by modeling the type of behavior that they need to model to the world.

- Correct bad behaviors promptly, but if you feel anger, calm down by praying to God before disciplining. During your private closet prayer moments, seek God for help with disciplining your children.

- Request that God reveal the talents, and/or gifts of the Spirit that your children may already possess, and ask Him for ways to help them live out their three purposes (love God, love others, and be disciples).

- Formulate a daily structure time for God with your stage 1 children, journal your experiences, and always make your time in the Vine fun!

CHAPTER 5

"You Will Bear Much Fruit"

Part 4: Stage 2 or Teaching Level (Walls)

Jesus states:

> I AM THE VINE; YOU ARE THE BRANCHES. IF YOU
> REMAIN IN ME AND I IN YOU, YOU WILL BEAR MUCH
> FRUIT; APART FROM ME YOU CAN DO NOTHING.
> (JOHN 15:5 NIV)

Stage: 2	Parenting Level: Teaching (Walls)	Ages: 7–11
Next, it's time to add the walls. If the foundation is in place properly, it can be good support for the walls. This is stage 2 or the Teaching Level. The walls define the meaning of the foundation. If assembled properly, the walls will be built around a Chief Cornerstone (Jesus) that will protect the dwelling.		

Why didn't we know that being parents would mean that our title would have a multitude of meanings? There are too many to list here, but one of our most infamous ones is "the teacher." Before we proceed, let me remind you that if you have a child that is between the ages of seven and eleven but that has not been taught about the love of Jesus or received a strong godly foundation, then you may want to begin at stage 1. Omit anything that you feel is no longer appropriate for your child's age category from stage 1, but it is highly recommend that children first obtain a solid foundation before proceeding to stage 2.

Once the foundation has been built, it is time to teach! You will likely teach a lot during this phase of their lives. Before you know it, they will be teenagers, so it's time to prepare them to be able to handle many things in life so they can function on their own someday. Though you have hopefully been teaching your child all along, it's now time to protect that love of Christ. Ensure that your children maintain their current godly structures, but now you can start to engage in more in-depth conversations about the Bible, God, Jesus, the Holy Spirit, and Satan.

This is the age that they will start to engage in more relationships outside of those confined within their homes. They will start to hear and experience more. The world will begin to look a little differently than the happy life that they have hopefully been experiencing. It's time to invest in a new age-appropriate Bible for this age group. Begin to read and discuss it together. Relate some of the biblical stories to life experiences. This will bring an awareness that the Bible leads them to the proper way to handle daily occurrences. When they experience issues with friends or at school, make sure you first pray together, then, occasionally, role play fun ways to handle the situations. Use Bible stories that relate to their particular issues as a way to educate them as to why God's ways don't correlate with the ways of the world. Help them recite scriptures that relate to their particular circumstances, and teach them how to meditate on the Word and draw strength from these verses.

Teach them how their fruit of the Spirit is so valuable to the kingdom. This is a great age group to start recognizing the strength of their character more than their achievements. Meaning if they bring home an A, say things such as, "Whoop, whoop, that's my girl! You maintained your structures for the Lord, studied hard, finished your homework, and brought home an A!"

Bold Parenting

It's time to become bold parents! This age group must understand why they can't see a certain movie, listen to a certain song, or join a certain social group. Make sure you guard their little eyes and ears as much as possible. What they are taking in is what they are receiving! Avoid music with sexual messages or inappropriate language. It's a good idea to make sure that spiritually uplifting messages are within at least 60 percent of the songs that are in their musical devices. Music should soothe the soul not corrupt it. Remember Satan wants to work his way into their minds, and music is a powerful method that he uses! Unfortunately, the majority of their friends may not be listening to an appropriate style of music; that is why it is so important to teach them why you are not allowing them to listen to some of the secular songs.

Make sure your children have a fun life in the Vine. Laugh a lot, play with them, and enjoy life. While we were being goof balls around the house, I would often "sneak in" teaching moments. I tried to prepare our son for the future by providing insight into some of the changes or temptations that some children may experience within the upcoming year. Since we were once young too, as parents, we can often relate to their situations and perceive some challenges ahead of them. There is power in giving our children that type of future insight because it helps them to understand that they are normal, prepares them for what to expect, creates ways to handle situations, and arms them with ways to minister to their friends who may start to experience some worldly temptations.

Think about it! Wouldn't you like to know what might happen within the next year? This information allowed our son to trust us and regard us as a knowledgeable source. If those things we had mentioned came to fruition, it wasn't much of a shock to him.

He would often tell me what his friends were being steered toward. Along with those discussions, I would reference this Bible verse and his purposes on this earth.

Jesus said:

> Enter through the narrow gate. For wide is the gate and broad is the road that leads to destruction, and many enter through it. But small is the gate and narrow the road that leads to life, and only a few find it. (Matthew 7:13-14 NIV)

Our son began to detest the negative changes he saw in his friends. Due to our talks and our prayers for him, he began to understand how Satan attempts to use temptations of this world to mislead him and his friends. There were years when he was upset with me for not buying many violent video games, but through prayer, the Spirit has allowed him to understand.

I regret purchasing some video games that were slightly inappropriate, but I am thankful that God showed me how to address those mistakes that I made previously. Some of the games my son owned were thrown into the trash, while others that I may not be fond of, he is still allowed to play. Since all of our children are different, we must be led by the Spirit to boldly do whatever God leads us to do. Always seek God to uncover the areas that Satan may be attempting to lure your child into in the hopes of someday destroying them. Some attacks may be visible to you, but all will be visible to God. Maintain your connection with Jesus, and by doing so, the Holy Spirit in due time may reveal things to you. One Christian father may feel that it is okay for his son to play a boxing video game. However, there may be another Christian father who has a child showing signs of violence, so that particular father may be led to not allow his son to play boxing games any longer. Let's not judge one another as parents but pray for each other to be convicted by the Holy Spirit. If we do all we can to demonstrate the fruit of the Spirit to other parents, they may be led to build a relationship with Christ and begin to do what is best for their children.

Adding the "Walls"

By the time your children reach stage 2, with assistance, they should be able to start writing in their own biblical journals. When you notice a blessing or a prayer being answered, excitedly ask them to write it in their journals. At times, entice them to read their journal entries to you. Imagine them reading while you curl up together with a soft blanket and drink some hot chocolate. Can't you just visualize your baby reading what God has done for him or her?

Now that warms the heart more than the hot chocolate!

Teach them the different ways to pray and train them to lead prayers and get them accustomed to praying for others. Tell them your age-appropriate stories about your life and your walk with God. Let them know what God has done for you. By this time, you may have observed some of their talents starting to surface. Really seek God for ways to use their abilities for the kingdom. Remain aware of the fruit of the Spirit and point out characteristics that you see in them that would be pleasing to the Lord.

Teach your children to be aware of the needs of others. Make sure you discuss the meaning of tithing and ensure they do it weekly. Include your child in outreach ministries and invite their friends. It may be as simple as occasionally sitting and talking with an elderly person about his or her life and/or growth with the Lord. Perhaps it can be as involved as preparing food to be distributed to a homeless shelter.

If you continue to live a life that demonstrates the fruit of the Spirit with the desired results to live out your purposes, you will feel true joy, which comes from God. Anytime that you are giving, make sure God's grace is shown in the event. Praise God for His love, give a testimony, or let your children read a Bible verse that either of you are led to share with the receiving individual. Let the Holy Spirit guide the process of discipleship. Anytime that you have helped others or shared God's goodness, explain all the works of the Lord that were visible within those encounters and ask your children to journal the events so they can hold on to the joy of helping others.

Hopefully, by this age, you will start to see your children confessing Christ and desiring to be baptized! They should also begin to develop some spiritual friendships. Involve them in social activities that enhance their abilities to meet other Christ followers within this age group. Make sure they firmly understand the meaning of the cross and what Jesus did for us on that special day. You may notice more spiritual gifts being given to your children. This will be a sign to you that God is working in them, and the fruit of the Spirit will be a sign to the world that the Spirit of God lives in them!

If possible, set aside some type of individual alone time for each of your children daily. Family dinnertime is great, but try to ensure that you have some alone time with each child because many children may not reveal personal matters in front of the entire family at one setting. When you are having this alone time, do something that he or she enjoys together, and you will likely uncover many things that are going on in the child's life. Sometimes children may reveal spiritual attacks that are being waged against them or their friends.

If you cannot set aside this alone time daily, start a particular ritual that you do with your child on a weekly basis. You will thank me for this once he or she becomes a teen because that's when some children pull away from parents. However, if you have maintained a close relationship throughout his or her life, it's likely that the internal child will secretly desire that special moment with you—hence creating that bond forever. I have been blessed with the ability to spend a good amount of alone time with each of our children daily; on the other hand, my husband has found that he and my son bond better over a plate of chicken wings, so they attempt to eat out without us girls once a week.

The main objective within this age group is to build upon the foundation. By now, you should start to see your children moving deeper into a life in the Vine. You are adding the walls around Christ. Your job is to protect that love of Him. Satan wants to break down the walls so that he can attempt to snatch the love of Christ out. You have to teach in a way that reaches your particular child. You still have a strong impact with your child. Your impact is greater than the impact of the world, but, unfortunately, it may not remain that way if you don't invest the time and teach now.

The table below gives a visual representation of some of the *structures* that you may want to put in place daily for this age group. The *fruit* is a reminder of the characteristics that parents should strive to model daily within and outside their home. Many parents believe that sibling rivalry is normal. You may have observed siblings directing some very hurtful comments toward one another while the parents sat idle. Teach your children to observe the fruit of the Spirit by exemplifying those traits within the home. Kids will have disagreements, but parents should never tolerate hurtful comments deliberately aimed toward one another. Stand firm on this topic because your home is their preparation for life.

Use the table below as an example. The *talents and attributes* are just examples of traits that you may notice in your children. Whatever you notice, pray about ways to use what God has shown you for the kingdom. The gifts category represent *spiritual gifts* from God that believers receive. Some of you may have begun to notice them in your children. However, many may not experience these until much later in life or even adulthood. The *purposes* column never changes. It is your ultimate goal for your children. It is achieved by you teaching your children how to maintain their structures, modeling Christ's behaviors, and God will handle the rest.

Ages 7 – 11 Years (Teaching)				
Structures + Fruits + Talents + Gifts = 3 Purposes				
Structures	Fruits	Talents & Attributes	Gifts	Purposes
Attend church weekly	Love	Artistic	Faith	Love the Lord our God with all our heart and with all our soul and with all our mind
Read age appropriate Bible daily	Joy	Leader	Wisdom	Love others as we love ourselves.
Listen to spiritually uplifting music daily	Peace	Sociably appealing	Knowledge	Make Disciples (Help others have a relationship with our Lord)
Daily Prayer Time	Patience	Witty or Entertaining	Healing	
Tithing and Giving	Kindness	Determined	Miraculous Powers	
Journaling	Goodness	Energetic	Prophecy	
Outreach Ministry Involvement	Faithfulness	Motivational	Distinguishing between spirits	
Talk about God, Jesus & the Holy Spirit daily	Gentleness	Inspiring	Speaking in different tongues	
Share stories to build Faith	Self-control	Imaginative	Distinguishing between different tongues	

Use this table to fill in the talents and any gifts of the Spirit that you may notice in your stage 2 children. If you have more than two stage 2 children, make copies of this chart. Write their names on the front. Remember to pray for God to reveal ways in which your family's life may bless others. Record your experiences in your journals!

Ages 7–11 Years (Teaching)				
Structures + Fruits + Talents + Gifts = 3 Purposes				
Structures	Fruits	Examples of Talents and Attributes	Gifts	Purposes
Attend church weekly	Love			Love the Lord our God with all our hearts and with all our souls and with all our minds
Read age-appropriate Bible daily	Joy			Love others as we love ourselves
Listen to spiritually uplifting music daily	Peace			Be disciples (help others have a relationship with our Lord)
Daily prayer time	Patience			
Tithing and giving	Kindness			
Journaling	Goodness			
Outreach ministry involvement	Faithfulness			
Talk about God, Jesus, and the Holy Spirit daily	Gentleness			
Share stories to build faith	Self-control			

Use this table to fill in the talents and any gifts of the Spirit that you may notice in your stage 2 children. If you have more than two stage 2 children, make copies of this chart. Write their names on the front. Remember to pray for God to reveal ways in which your family's life may bless others. Record your experiences in your journals!

Ages 7–11 Years (Teaching)				
Structures + Fruits + Talents + Gifts = 3 Purposes				
Structures	Fruits	Examples of Talents and Attributes	Gifts	Purposes
Attend church weekly	Love			Love the Lord our God with all our hearts and with all our souls and with all our minds!
Read age-appropriate Bible daily	Joy			Love others as we love ourselves
Listen to spiritually uplifting music daily	Peace			Be disciples (help others have a relationship with our Lord)
Daily prayer time	Patience			
Tithing and giving	Kindness			
Journaling	Goodness			
Outreach ministry involvement	Faithfulness			
Talk about God, Jesus, and the Holy Spirit daily	Gentleness			
Share stories to build faith	Self-control			

CHAPTER 5

"You Will Bear Much Fruit"

Part 4: Stage 2 or Teaching Level (Walls)
Summary

Jesus states:

> I AM THE VINE; YOU ARE THE BRANCHES. IF YOU
> REMAIN IN ME AND I IN YOU, YOU WILL BEAR MUCH
> FRUIT; APART FROM ME YOU CAN DO NOTHING.
> (JOHN 15:5 NIV)

- Stage 2 is when parents begin to build upon their children's godly foundation by adding "the Walls" of protection around Christ.

- During this stage, it's important to use the Bible to explain God's ways versus the world's ways, and then to use biblical stories to support why God's Word is the truth.

- Encourage your children to document their godly experiences in their journals. Ask them to read them to you while you cuddle together. You are creating good memories and positive emotional feelings about God and His love for them.

- Ensure their Vine time is fun and put in place daily.

- If possible, make alone time for each of your children daily by doing something he or she enjoys. This will help you build your relationship, maintain your connection with your child, prepare him or her for the future, and uncover spiritual attacks in his or her lives and the lives of his or her friends.

- Help them form godly friendships by involving them in church activities.

- Appropriately prepare them for temptations and changes that children may notice within the upcoming year. Discuss plans of Satan and how to handle certain situations. Always encourage them to discuss their concerns with God and with you.

- Pray about beginning a discipleship outreach routine, and include their friends if possible.

CHAPTER 5

"You Will Bear Much Fruit"

Part 5: Stage 3 or Coaching Level (Bricks)

Jesus states:

> I AM THE VINE; YOU ARE THE BRANCHES. IF YOU REMAIN IN ME AND I IN YOU, YOU WILL BEAR MUCH FRUIT; APART FROM ME YOU CAN DO NOTHING. (JOHN 15:5 NIV)

Stage: 3	Parenting Level: Coaching (Bricks)	Ages: 12–18
Stage 3 is the Coaching Level. This is when the bricks will be added to provide stability. The bricks may receive some damages from a few strong winds. Therefore, the builders (parents), may need to make some adjustments, so that the house is formed to withstand some powerful storms ahead.		

If the earlier years were built on a solid foundation, and the walls are protecting the dwelling of the Holy Spirit, then it's a good idea to increase your prayers for your children as your personal involvement decreases. It's time to become coaches! Between the ages of twelve to fourteen, parents can still provide some teaching combined with coaching. However, by the time kids are around sixteen, I mean let's face it, is there really anything that they don't know? I mean really, people.

Oftentimes, parents are starting to feel like roadway engineers that are holding up signs trying to direct the flow of traffic, yet their children may turn toward the wrong path. This often leads parents to feel as though their children are headed toward a dead end or, even worse, "the Pit." A lot is coming at children during this phase of their lives. Some of their alternate personality characteristics may be due to hormonal issues, peer pressure, insecurities, and desires to be independent. Others are due to an increase in the number of attacks Satan is pounding on them. Many parents may arrive here wondering what in the world happened to their child that sat on their lap reading journals and drinking hot chocolate.

Well, they are still in there; however, time to prepare them for a life in the Vine really is of the essence. Many children may leave home right after this stage, so parents must become very inspirational coaches. When you have the power of the Holy Spirit and have invested time in your children over the years, you know their souls, so you can coach them in a meaningful and impactful way! Sometimes, regardless of all the things parents have done, I have still heard stories of even some pastors' children turning far away from the Lord during this stage. You see, Satan wants a child of a godly person more than he wants a sinner's child because a child trained to make Jesus Lord over his or her life grows and becomes fruitful, which is detrimental for Satan's plans. When children whose lives were built upon the foundation of the Lord are struggling and acting out, the Spirit of God pulls on them and causes mental anguish. It is hard for them to stay in a life of sin. So keep praying and coaching. This battle is God's to win; fortunately, you are on the right team!

I once heard Joyce Meyer talk about how she was angry with her teenage son because he wasn't living the life of Christ that she wanted him to live. One day, she had a revelation to just forgive her son and apologize to him for the times in which she had not been forgiving and understanding. When she did that, he cried and told her that he wanted to experience God in the way that she had, but he just hadn't yet. Later, her son changed and became a valuable part of her remarkable ministry.

I love that story because I think many parents have not forgiven their children for not being "godly enough" or for their mistakes. You can imagine the frustration that sets in when a parent has spent many years training their children about God, yet their children's characteristics contradict their parental teachings. Those parents probably begin to reevaluate what they did or didn't do, and guilt starts to build up in their hearts. All of this is a spiritual attack by Satan! You cannot change anyone or alter the past, so the best thing for a grieving parent to do is to stop worrying, blaming themselves, or doubting. Just put it in the hands of God, and trust in His awesome ability to intercede. I sometimes think of all the mistakes in my life, yet, due to God's grace, I still made my way to Christ. There is a testimony through the process of establishing a connection to Jesus, so rejoice in what's ahead as you keep modeling the behavior of Christ!

He Huffed and Puffed But Couldn't Blow the Brick House Down

Believe me, Satan will be huffing and puffing trying to destroy what you and Christ built in your children, so keep focusing on the daily godly structures. If they are still living inside your home, remember Joshua's old saying that goes: But as for me and my household, we will serve the Lord (Joshua 24:15, summarizing). It is so important for children to learn how to talk with God and allow Him to teach through their prayer time and life's experiences. Make sure that you find ways to communicate with your children as often as possible. Now is the time to encourage your kids to set their own Vine time, but ask them occasionally about what they read in their Bibles. It is also a good idea to have a weekly family Bible study time. During the ages of seven to eleven, parents were expected to start a daily or weekly ritual with their children. If you have not as of yet, please start it now! Pick up a hobby or something that they enjoy doing, and do it with them. Please make this your priority! This will often create extra time to talk and maintain bonds. Make sure this fun time includes a discussion about God, faith, and life. Pray for them to build godly friendships with others in this age category and help them form outreach ministries with their friends. This will form accountabilities of their purposes and promote a lifelong desire to be disciples among them and their peers.

Children are trying to find a meaning or a purpose for themselves during this phase of their lives. They are uncertain about so much and may even be concerned about their futures. That is why it is imperative to spend the first part of their lives acquainting them with their true purposes. Once that acknowledgment is established, and they grow in the meaning of it, they can appreciate who they are because they know who they belong to is far greater than anything in this world. Increasing their outreach ministry as they approach their teenage years gives them a way to do God's work and demonstrate to the world how to live by the fruit of the Spirit. You may be able to find trusted local community outreach opportunities in your area in which children can take part. That type of training gives them a greater purpose and promotes internal peace and joy.

What Is a Coach?

You may be wondering, so what does a coach do exactly? A coach is more of a strategic teacher. The game of life is now beginning. A coach (parent) has advanced from being a player because a parent is not able to go out and be an active participate in the game anymore. The coach is there for direction and strategizing. By the time your child has reached this stage, he or she should be establishing his or her own life in the Vine. You are there to ensure that his or her race to the kingdom is progressing in the right direction. As the parent, you may see obstacles ahead. That is the time to pray for God's direction, and let the Holy Spirit guide you toward a method of persuasion. Then you can provide information about the obstacle and how it can affect children's purposes. Once you see wisdom within your children, start allowing them to make some choices about things. At times, you may want to transition your teaching style from a direct no to asking them what they think is best and why. Remember you are preparing them for life and the ability to make their own decisions. You have spent stage 2 teaching them right from wrong and about God's love. Now it's time for you to let them make some choices while you coach them how to do it.

When we first started training our son during stage 3, he found a song that he wanted to purchase. He approached me with the video of the song on his phone and asked if I would purchase it. I looked down at the video and saw some scenes I didn't think were quite appropriate. I think the video may have included a robbery. All I knew was that it was secular music, and it didn't appear to have a righteous purpose. I know how Satan is looking for any small crack to get into this house that we are building (spiritual son). Our son said that he just liked the beat of the song. My brain was shouting, "*No, you can't buy that song!*" However, realizing that I was in the coaching phase, and since the song probably wasn't too bad, I decided to use this as a coaching opportunity. So, I said,

"Why don't you listen to it again? Pray about it, and then tell me if you think I should invest our money toward that song." Of course, I was really depending upon my Father in Heaven to help me out here. Later that day, our son came in and said, "I don't think God would like you to buy that song." *Yippee! God is so good.*

Now, that isn't always the approach to use in the coaching phase. You have to let the Holy Spirit allow you to use good judgment. We still had to say no quite often, but I provided better explanations and alternative methods. We were working toward training our son how to make his own righteous decisions. I couldn't have left many decisions in his hands if he had not started to receive wisdom from the Lord.

It's important for parents to enhance their parenting style as their children grow and develop. If the parents' approach never changes, children will often rebel more easily and attempt to demolish most of the good teachings of their parents as soon as possible. They only see worldly freedom ahead. They never realize that Jesus provided their freedom. Another reason that children may rebel may be due to a harsh reaction from their parents when they uncovered a sin that was part of their child's life. Pray for God to provide wisdom as to how to handle situations, but attempt to control your emotions in front of your children.

Sometimes a child may feel badly about something he or she did and confess it to his or her parents. If possible, when your child attempts to discuss something with you, try to be receptive and understanding, especially if he or she didn't have to tell you. The child may be learning to value your spiritual input, or the Holy Spirit may be pulling them toward repentance. Handle this situation with grace, but seek God for guidance. Praise their wisdom (gift) to recognize that it was a sin; praise them for discussing it with you, and then move toward resolving the situation. Remember, you never want your child to feel like he or she cannot talk to you. Think of the number of times, we had to repent before our Father in Heaven.

Stage 3 and the following stage require a lot of praying over your children. Also, remember to bless them. In addition to that, pray for God to steer them away from temptations and deceptions of the enemy. Remember, day by day, you are placing the bricks on the home to withstand some of the outer elements. Hopefully, the Spirit of God has found its dwelling place inside this new home. Your job is to keep placing those bricks, preparing the house to stand and stand firmly!

CHAPTER 5

"You Will Bear Much Fruit"

Part 5: Stage 3 or Coaching Level (Bricks)
Summary

Jesus states:

> I AM THE VINE; YOU ARE THE BRANCHES. IF YOU
> REMAIN IN ME AND I IN YOU, YOU WILL BEAR MUCH
> FRUIT; APART FROM ME YOU CAN DO NOTHING.
> (JOHN 15:5 NIV)

- Stage 3 is the Coaching Level. By the time kids are becoming teenagers, it is time for them to learn how to make godly choices on their own.

- Prior to Stage 3, they should have learned their three purposes in life thus enabling them to form an eternal rather than a temporal mind-set. Meaning, they understand that this world isn't their final home, so their most important choices should be based upon things that last forever (God, reaching heaven, and helping others along the way).

- Parents must accept the fact that children will make mistakes. There is a process to obtaining a maturity in Christ. All of us are going through it. Be forgiving.

- Make sure that your children learn how to pray, meditate, and study God's Word daily. The Holy Spirit can speak to them through the Word. Oftentimes, a revelation may occur when the Word aligns with your coaching. This will help establish their growth, maturity, and wisdom.

- Stage 3 is like adding the bricks to a home. The brick analogy is like solidifying a protection around the love of Christ. Satan will likely attack your children more aggressively now. However, the bricks that you are placing around the love of Christ will help to secure His dwelling.

- A coach is merely a strategic teacher. God is with you on this journey, and He wants to order your steps!

CHAPTER 5

"You Will Bear Much Fruit"

Part 6: Stage 4 or Advising/Friendship Level (Roof)

Jesus states:

> I AM THE VINE; YOU ARE THE BRANCHES. IF YOU REMAIN IN ME AND I IN YOU, YOU WILL BEAR MUCH FRUIT; APART FROM ME YOU CAN DO NOTHING. (JOHN 15:5 NIV)

Stage 4:	Parenting Level: Advising or Friendship (Roof)	Ages: 19 and Up (Adulthood)
Lastly is stage 4 or the Advising Level. The roof will be added establishing its completeness. Gradually, the builders (parents) will begin to walk away. The builders will check on the home and will never fully abandon its creation. Though the home will likely need some repairs here and there, if Jesus, the Chief Cornerstone, has found His dwelling inside the home, it will last forever (eternity)!		

Discipline, teaching, and coaching do not require an open invitation; however, you have to earn the ability to be an adviser. Due to the fact that their child may still be living under their roof, or they may be paying for their child's college tuition, many parents think that they should still be making an impact with their children. If you do not have a personal relationship established with your adult child, you are attempting to train a stage 4 young adult by using a disciplinary or teaching approach. This typically won't work! That doesn't mean that you relinquish your rules, because your children must still respect authority and follow the proper rules that you have set forth; yet, you should transition toward a friendship role with your stage 4 child, so that he or she will be able to mentally accept your advice.

Ensuring that your children desire to talk to you is just as important as ensuring that they continue to follow your rules. This balancing is not easy; however, once again it is all about your approach. The fruit of the Spirit is the key to your effectiveness. Pray for the ability to reach your children. I have talked to many parents that have young adult children, and, I must say, stage 4 is the age that parents begin the process of reevaluating their parental skills. Mental questions start surfacing, such as, "Did I spend enough time with Little Johnny, or did I teach him enough to make it on his own?" When children become adults, parents often have many areas of concerns for their children, but their ability to reverse negative behaviors in the natural sense has often declined greatly.

Worldly Priorities or Godly Priorities?

Most parents have made their child's social status and grades their priority, or they made God their priority. It is easy to determine the one that you focused upon the most by selecting the statement below that would give you the greatest pleasure concerning your child's future.

- Your happiness surrounding your child would primarily be due to the fact that your child is studious, kind, well-rounded, talented, or independent.

- Your happiness surrounding your child would primarily be due to the fact that your child has been trained that Jesus needs to be Lord over all his or her situations in life.

Both of those statements are great and very important, but if your happiness is geared more toward the first statement, your child has probably established one of those characteristics as his or her priority in life. He or she may be prepared for a worldly success but not prepared to make godly choices or to handle the pain of this world. Let me share a story about a set of parents that selected statement 1.

I am going to call this stage 4 child Jessica. Jessica was raised to be polite and kind to others. All of her life her parents ensured that her good grades were the priority. Not only did her parents tell her that, but she also had a loving family that held her accountable to doing well in school. She went to church on Sundays, yet no one held her accountable to God. When they used the phrase "successful in life," they referenced her grades. Through many conversations with family members, Jessica received extensive training about the importance of making a lot of money. She was taking it all in and was determined that she would become very successful in life.

After Jessica graduated from college and obtained a great job, she was making more money than both her parents combined. She began to purchase things of high quality that demonstrated her rise to success. Everyone was so proud of her! Though she visited her parents on holidays, she gradually stopped talking to them regularly. They barely knew what was happening in her life. Her parents' income declined greatly, but Jessica didn't offer to help much. She was busy traveling to exotic locations around the world. They didn't even know when she was working or on vacation. Shortly after disconnecting from her parents, she stopped going to church because ... well, she just no longer saw the need.

When Jessica was around various family members, they all bragged on her worldly achievements. This solidified her pride in herself. When either of her parents tried to talk to her about God, she would stop that conversation immediately. She told them that she didn't have to go to church to have a relationship with God and proceeded to tell them that her relationship with God was none of their business anyway. Her pride was even beginning to remove the respect for her parents that was such a profound part of her character. Her image of success had been obtained. She even began to look at her parents differently because since they were no longer of any financial use to her, their value in her eyes had declined.

These became her thoughts: *Life is good. Why do I really need God?* She would give to people if she desired. She believed in God and could occasionally pray for someone if he or she was ill or in crisis. What was the point in developing a meaningful relationship with the Lord? She was in charge of her own life. It was her abilities that led her to success. She worked hard, and now she was about to enjoy life and fully indulge in the excitement this world has to offer!

What could Jessica's parents do at this point? Though they might have been able to clearly see the ways they should have trained their child differently, how could their training be reversed? Guilt wanted to take ownership within their hearts. Yet, holding on to guilt and worry was just a fleshly type of thinking, meaning that if they replayed their mistakes and held on to the guilt long enough, they might be able to form a solution. That was not the way to handle this situation. Satan wanted to use guilt and frustration to keep Jessica's parents in bondage by creating hostility between her and them. However, Jesus came to free us from guilt through repentance. It was time for them to repent to God for their mistakes, forgive Jessica, and ask God to remove the guilt from their hearts and minds so they could begin to allow the Holy Spirit to change the situation.

Jessica's parents lost the ability to raise her to have a life in the Vine, and their ability to advise may have seemed dismal, but with God all things are possible. Her parents' prayers were their most powerful weapon against the spirit of pride that was consuming Jessica. They had to pray for their child daily and for God to give them spiritual wisdom as to how to advise her. They needed to reestablish a solid relationship with Jessica by seeking God to help them build one. Sometimes it's hard for parents to even enjoy the company of this type of child; yet, as I believe the Spirit of God once said to me, "It's not about you!" As parents, we must make the decision that the extensions of our branches will flourish with fruit; so don't allow Satan's deceptions to affect your ability to be an effective advising parent!

As you are rebuilding a relationship with your child, you may have to place yourself where your child is in life. Become empathetic as to how he or she arrived at whatever mental state he or she seems to be in at this moment. You need to establish an ability to be an adviser by first becoming forgiving, less judgmental, and his or her friend. Sometimes it's harder to forgive those closest to us than it is a stranger because the depth of that hurt can be stronger, so pray for the grace to be like Jesus. Oftentimes, parents try to shame their children closer to God, but consistently seeing God in you may be the very thing that entices them to change.

Though your child's life may seem so perfect for him or her, God has a way of moving people closer to Him. My son once said, "Life is like a little toy car that you have to pull back so that it can zoom forward. If we are no longer moving toward God, He may have to pull us back a little so that we can really zoom!" I hope you got that.

The best way to reach an adult child is to listen to him or her. Allow your encounters to be filled with the fruit of the Spirit. Create an environment of love that entices him or her to want to get closer to you and God. Share some of your testimonies when they are in line with the topic of discussion. The adult child will likely start to listen to you if you have been primarily listening to him or her. Pray for the Holy Spirit to work through and intercede in your child's life by creating ways those seeds may be watered, thereby establishing roots. God can take your words and turn them into a revelation through experiences within your child's life.

Believe me, the adult children will need the Lord! You want them to go to God. However, if they are enticed to come to you, you can help direct them to God. You probably wish that you could just hold up a road map sign that says, "This way to God!" However, if your child feels she can talk to you without condemnation and judgment, your life in the Vine becomes her road map.

If you are having a difficult time visualizing what advising looks like, then imagine that you are seeking some advice from a previous employer whom you really respect. Your previous employer may likely say something such as, "Do you mind if I share something that worked in my life?" Once you value the opinion of someone of authority, you welcome him or her to provide direction and guidance.

If your adult child has no respect for you or your opinion, but still relies upon you in some way, pray and seek help from a spiritual counselor or pastor and make the necessary decision as to how to proceed with a relationship with your adult child. Refuse to be led to "the Pit" with anyone. Your life is precious and deserves joy, so do what you can to protect your adult child, but don't let anyone come between you and your relationship with Christ.

God may have to discipline your children in order for them to realize they need Him. Seek God before you continue to rescue a child that is traveling down the same road of destruction. They may have to get to a dead end before they desire to find an alternate route. Let God order all your steps!

Keep having faith because God is amazing! I wish that I had good news to share about the person that I am calling Jessica, but not yet. We are praying for this situation. I want to tell her parents that if they don't believe God can fix it, then look at me; if they still don't believe He can fix it, then look at them!

Godly Priorities!

Remember these two statements that would give you the greatest pleasure concerning your child's future? Well, if you selected statement 2 as the one that would give you the greatest sense of pleasure, then your child probably would exemplify characteristics of statements 1 and 2.

- Your happiness surrounding your child would primarily be due to the fact that your child is studious, kind, well-rounded, talented, or independent.

- Your happiness surrounding your child would primarily be due to the fact that your child has been trained that Jesus needs to be Lord over all his/her situations in life.

If your happiness surrounding your child is due to the fact that your child has been trained to make Jesus Lord over all his or her situations in life, then God has likely blessed your child to also be studious, kind, well-rounded, talented, independent, and so much more!

When you have this type of adult child, celebrate! Your house has been built! You are adding the roof. A synonym sometimes used for roof is crown.

> Everyone who competes in the games goes into strict training. They do it to get a crown that will not last; but we do it to get a crown that will last forever. (1 Corinthians 9:25 NIV)

Rejoice in the fact that your child has a righteous crown.

Though your children may be starting the right path of life, continue to pray for them and their relationship with Jesus and others throughout their lives. They will need those prayers more than ever. Every house's roof gets a leak every once in a while. During this stage of parenthood, make sure you maintain a close friendship with your young adult child. Sometimes it is difficult to accomplish this when your child is transitioning from teenage years to young adulthood. If possible, try to maintain outreach missions to do together periodically. If not, encourage him or her to find a local group of young adults from church that he or she can partner with to share God's love within the community. Understand that oftentimes your child desires to be treated fully like an adult but still may need your financial support. Parents are often quick to remind them that they are not adults until they can stand firmly on their own. It is especially challenging when this age group is living in your home (godly or not) and is expecting to come and go as they wish. Remain firm on your unwavering rules. However, think honestly about some of your expectations for them, and decide if there are a few areas (God willing) where you can be more lenient.

Remember, when you are an advising parent, you should learn to be more of a listener than a talker. There may be times where you can share some of your past stories that relate to some of their issues. Tell them how you overcame them or where you went wrong. If they think that you are perfect and never made mistakes, it may deter them from talking with you about their struggles. Of course, you may not want to share all of your transgressions. Become a wise confidant and friend. I have had parents say to me, "I am not my child's friend no matter what age they may be approaching." Even God wants to be our friend; yet He is still our Father in Heaven.

> And the scripture was fulfilled that says, "Abraham believed God, and it was credited to him as righteousness," and he was called God's friend. (James 2:23 NIV)

Parenting is not about dominating our children. It is about loving them and training them to know the Lord in such a way that they can become one of His and your dearest friends. Their lives will be enriched because you have taught them to know that they can rely upon His strength when they feel they have depleted all of their own! Teach them that whenever their strength is gone, they should *rejoice* because they are about to tap into the *all powerful strength of God*!

Success in Life

Please understand that there are many things that determine success. Financial success is one of them. It is important to teach our children to do well in this life. However, the evil spirits that are among us in this world are always roaming to devour us. If we only stand upon our own capabilities, we cannot stand long. It is imperative that we demonstrate a life in the Vine to our children. Then they will not only make it to the kingdom someday, but they will also learn how to survive the daily trials of this world. Keep promoting hard work and perseverance, but keep referencing God because He provides the strength. Once your houses have been formed and the Spirit of God is shining through them, your children won't be able to keep Him to themselves. They will start proactively sharing the love of God with others and someday with their own children.

Enjoy your fruitful harvest!

CHAPTER 5

"You Will Bear Much Fruit"

Part 6: Stage 4 or Advising/Friendship Level (Roof)
Summary

Jesus states:

> I AM THE VINE; YOU ARE THE BRANCHES. IF YOU
> REMAIN IN ME AND I IN YOU, YOU WILL BEAR MUCH
> FRUIT; APART FROM ME YOU CAN DO NOTHING.
> (JOHN 15:5 NIV)

- Stage 4 parenting is about learning how to become an advising parent. The analogy used to describe this is when the builders (parents) have completed the home and are adding the roof (crown) on the home. Everyone who competes in the games goes into strict training. They do it to get a crown that will not last; but we do it to get a crown that will last forever (1 Corinthians 9:25 NIV).

- The builders (parents) begin to walk away, but they will never fully abandon their home. Parents should remain in close relationship with their children, thereby becoming their friends once they reach stage 4.

- Seeing the fruit of the Spirit in you is the most effective way to demonstrate a life in the Vine.

- Don't try to shame your children closer to God, because consistently seeing God in you may be all they need to change.

- Share your mistakes, as appropriate, so they will understand your process of establishing a life in the Vine.

- Advise your children about the importance of making eternal things a priority over worldly or temporal things. When children learn how to focus on the eternal first and then the temporal, they may make godly choices, and the power of the Holy Spirit will be their comforter (counselor, helper, advocate, intercessor, strengthener, and standby). No one knows how to truly bless children like our Father in Heaven!

- The blessings seem to flow from heaven when we have persevered through learning how to put God (and our three purposes) first all while also working diligently to achieve worldly success.

CHAPTER 6

"Apart from Me You Can Do Nothing"

Jesus states:

> I AM THE VINE; YOU ARE THE BRANCHES. IF YOU
> REMAIN IN ME AND I IN YOU, YOU WILL BEAR MUCH
> FRUIT; APART FROM ME YOU CAN DO NOTHING.
> (JOHN 15:5 NIV)

Life Apart from the Vine Leads to No Life at All

Honestly, I no longer understand how I functioned so many years without allowing the Holy Spirit to direct my path in life. However, I now understand that I was never really functioning but just tolerating my discontented life. By the time I reached this chapter of book two, God had grown me even more. I sat amazed at what He can do in such a short period of time. When our son was young, he once asked, "Mom, what is there to do in heaven?" He kept thinking about his video games and his inability to take them with him. At the time, I didn't have an answer exactly, but I can tell you that now God has shown me a little bit about what heaven is like on earth. I once focused on the evil within this world, the stress of this life, the sicknesses, and the mental anguish. This may sound so odd to you, but I can now sit among some of our most troublesome moments and still be filled with joy just by treasuring the goodness of my Father in my heart. Though I am still concerned about nonbelievers, those who hurt, the violence in our world, people being deceived, and my own personal struggles, His greatness overshadows every concern and soars me into a mind-set of love, faith, joy, and hope for the future! If I am able to experience such a powerful feeling in this sinful world, heaven must send us into a shock wave of excitement and praise for our Father!

So how is the rest of the world functioning? How do they find joy within sorrow? How do they find peace among chaos? How do they maintain stability surrounding turmoil? They truly can't! Without the power of the Holy Spirit, a person *is* helpless when life looks helpless! All their perceived strength is in themselves or humankind. Now I am so glad that I no longer have to depend on myself, my husband, or anyone else around me in this life. I lean on my husband as the man God has chosen for me, and I believe in my abilities that God has given me to accomplish things in life; yet, my true confidence and strength is only in *God*! Losing a job didn't send us into panic mode—well, it didn't keep us there, Hee-hee! Seriously, we learned that when we are in close fellowship with God, He doesn't let His children go through anything without a purpose or a greater outcome. Even death is a greater outcome to a follower of Christ because heaven awaits us. Since He loves us, we don't need to worry about *anything* in this world because our Father created the world and everything in it, including you and me.

Now when people call me to counsel them about troublesome situations in their lives, I'm glad they've reached out to me, but what I really want to say is, "Just align your life with Christ and forget about it." Living a life in the Vine is really that simple, but getting to the realization of that is not that simple because Satan is fighting us every step of the way. Some of you may have noticed that when you started to get closer to God, you allowed something to pull you away again. You were probably so close to the breakthrough of true freedom of doubt and worry upon your life. God was probably about to demonstrate something powerful to you, but you didn't allow yourself to stay the course. We have to learn how to pray, listen to the Holy Spirit, become obedient to Him, let Him establish our faith, and retrain our thinking from our selfish desires to that of God. It is a process that takes time and obedience. The best way to reach a mature life in the Vine is obtained by making time for God, by studying His Word, attending a church that aligns with His Word, prayer/worship, and allowing Him to create a heart to love demonstrated by your willingness to become His disciples. As we are going through this journey, God calls us to lovingly help others get to that place of knowledge and wisdom.

I remember observing people who seemed to have it all but didn't have Christ. They had nice homes, cars, jobs, and beautiful families. I thought, *If Jesus says apart from Him we can't do anything, then how are all these people doing so much?* God then showed me what "doing" something meant. "Doing" something means to be fruitful or to produce something that is building up others, thereby building up the kingdom of God. God wants all of His people to realize that He will provide for us on this Earth. Satan wouldn't have been sent to Earth without us having the capability of defeating him. Even sickness and death can't destroy a Christian because we have a real life waiting for us! My mind is mine! Satan can't dominate it! Sure, he tries to affect it, but God sends me the wisdom to see what he is doing. Yet, I still must make a conscious effort every day to stay in the Vine so that I can receive strength from the Holy Spirit. God desires for us to be joyous and blessed. Our faith in Him is what produces the security that we are all searching for in this life. Our calling as fruitful Christians is to lovingly lead our children and God's people to the truth about Him. God told us to love others as we love ourselves, and the Holy Spirit allows us to be able to do it.

> Now, listen, you rich people, weep and wail because of the misery that is coming on you. Your wealth has rotted, and moths have eaten your clothes. Your gold and silver are corroded. Their corrosion will testify against you and eat your flesh like fire. You have hoarded wealth in the last days. (James 5:1–3 NIV)

God blesses many of His people with a vast amount of wealth, but when their hearts are aligning with Christ, they can't help but bless others as well. Though be careful of those who are living a sinful life yet are generous to others. Don't let their lifestyles confuse you into believing that because they give, their lifestyles have been accepted by Christ. God can bless people through any individual that He deems necessary, but good is only good when it is aligned with the will of God. Those of great wealth must be careful to not feel that their kindness will earn them a place in the kingdom of heaven, because Jesus paid the price for that on the cross. Don't allow fame of the rich or the desires of wealth to confuse or consume you. Please guard your mind and be watchful of Satan's tricks because we cannot choose to "live in sin," or our branches may snap.

As you train your children to remain in the Vine, enjoy your journey. I know I am! It's been eventful and exciting learning how to trust in our Father. You may be wondering if we ran out of money while I wrote book two. Well, of course not! Our Father has provided for us the entire time! Just as we were months away from our account appearing to be heading toward a negative balance, we decided to keep believing. Recently, our church leader (Pastor Rusty) told the story about the twelve spies in the Bible that went to check out the Promised Land for the Israelites (referencing Numbers 13 and 14). They returned to give a report. Ten basically said that for various reasons, they couldn't obtain the land that God had *already* promised. Yet, two (Joshua and Caleb) believed they could obtain the land. Well, guess what? The two that believed made it, but the ten that didn't died in the wilderness never being blessed by God's promise!

The day after I completed book two, I prayed to God asking Him for direction, and within hours of that prayer, I received a random phone call from a company within my career field asking me to fly to Texas the following week for a job interview.

Well …

I didn't get the job, but I had enough experiences with Christ to know that everything would be fine. Within a month, I received another phone call to fly to Texas for another interview.

Well …

I didn't get that job either; however, I was able to encourage and motivate others who were disappointed that they also didn't receive a job following that interview. I was completely fine and at peace.

A month or so later, I received another phone call for yet another job that I had not applied for, and this time I was to fly to New Jersey. Saint said, "I don't care if you get it or not because I know that regardless, God will take care of us!"

Well, guess what?

I got the job! Wow, look how God had grown our faith!

Saint and I decided to trust in God, so He faithfully provided for us! God is in control! He called me to write this book! His promise was fulfilled through my life! He gave me the words to do what I knew I didn't know how to do, but we chose to believe that He was more than capable of doing it through me!

There is nothing about me that is special except the fact that I am a child of God. So just as our Father is showing Himself through my family in a powerful way, He wants to do it for you too! As you journey through this life, continue the process of training your children and others to remain in the Vine so that your branches go beyond your inner circle and reach out into the world becoming an extension of Christ working through you and your children so that all of you will bear much fruit!

If there is anything that I hope you got out of this book, it's this: be led by the Holy Spirit, live by the fruit of the Spirit, study and believe in God's Word and His promises, make daily time for God, obtain your three purposes, and enjoy the process of training your children to remain in the Vine!

> Fix these words of mine in your hearts and minds; tie them as symbols on your hands and bind them on your foreheads. Teach them to your children, talking about them when you sit at home and when you walk along the road, when you lie down and when you get up. (Deuteronomy 11:18–19 NIV)

> Then Jesus came to them and said, "All authority in heaven and on earth has been given to me. Therefore go and make disciples of all nations, baptizing them in the name of the Father and of the Son and of the Holy Spirit, and teaching them to obey everything I have commanded you. And surely I am with you always, to the very end of the age." (Matthew 28:18–20 NIV)

May God bless your journey!

CHAPTER 6
"Apart from Me You Can Do Nothing"
Summary

Jesus states:

> I AM THE VINE; YOU ARE THE BRANCHES. IF YOU
> REMAIN IN ME AND I IN YOU, YOU WILL BEAR MUCH
> FRUIT; APART FROM ME YOU CAN DO NOTHING.
> (JOHN 15:5 NIV)

- Without the Spirit of God, we are weak and hopeless, because all of our capabilities are wrapped up in our own strength (and even that strength was formed by God).

- Jesus can provide joy during situations that would cause others to be consumed with worry and fear.

- Satan works diligently to prevent us from having a true revelation about the peace that comes from being fully attached to the Vine.

- Many people believe that a worldly success means that they are "doing" something. However, if those people's names are not written in the kingdom of heaven, their joy will only be temporary like all their possessions. Temporal is very short in comparison to forever (eternity).

- Be led by the Holy Spirit, live by the fruit of the Spirit, study and believe in God's Word and His promises, make daily time for God, obtain your three purposes, and enjoy the process of training your children to remain in the Vine!

May God bless your journey!

In Honor of Grandma Lee, Granddaddy, and Uncle Bubba

Reaping the Good Fruit

I spent most of my childhood looking inside my grandparents' kitchen window while playing among their swaying trees. The pinecones always awakened my bare feet with a shocking surprise. The scent of honeysuckle whispered across my nose following a playful breeze. There was an old, wooden box-shaped post assembled by hands just as timely. What a perfect place for entangled vines of grapes to dance and weave. I often pretended it was a shaded gazebo fit for a little princess. My uncle would sometimes give my little feet a boost in the air so that youthful fingers could reach for one of those sour delights. The breeze would shake the limbs of another, occasionally directing my attention to greenish-red apples falling to the ground. When a great wind surfaced, it enticed my petite arms to spread and direct a whimsical twirl while walnut, persimmon, and pear trees were all awaiting my visit. Just before I could pick the next special treat, I heard my grandma say, "It's time to plant the seeds."

My grandpa awakened that old tiller. It roared with a deafening sound. The smell of honeysuckle was replaced by the aroma of freshly cut grass. That old tiller ferociously shook my grandpa as it ripped into the soil. The soil began to break away while pieces of weeds flew into the air. Grandma grabbed an old jar filled with seeds and poured some into my delicate hands. She followed behind Grandpa with an old, rusty chopping hoe. I watched as her strong, aged hands dragged a line of deepened trenches into that soil. When I received a nod, I approached the first trench and placed a couple seeds within its cavity. I slowly continued down the row until I reached the end. Grandma then placed a few tiny particles of fertilizer on top of the seeds while I slipped away. Flip-flop was the sound of the water in my can as I was swiftly returning to Grandma so that I could pour it over our treasures. Then Grandma began to spread the fresh soil over the priceless seeds, burying them in the darkness of the earth.

Underground, roots were developing though they were unseen by impatient little eyes. Would they ever grow? What would the seeds produce? My grandpa said to keep caring for them the way you are told, and they will produce good fruit. Finally, after countless times of watering, hours of sunlight, days of tending to the soil, emerging patience, and my inherited tenacity, I noticed green leaves were sprouting from the mystery of the soil. I was about to reap what I sowed.

Through it all there is a lesson to be told. Though we are responsible for the sowing, without God's production of the soil, seed, water, and the sun, there would be no good fruit.

Jesus said:

I am the true vine, and my Father is the gardener. He cuts off every branch in me that bears no fruit, while every branch that does bear fruit he prunes so that it will be even more fruitful. You are already clean because of the word I have spoken to you. Remain in me, and I will remain in you. No branch can bear fruit by itself; it must remain in the vine. Neither can you bear fruit unless you remain in me. (John 15:1–4 NIV)

Thank You, Jesus!

ABOUT THE AUTHOR

Terita St. Julian is a wife and a mother who devoted her life to God, heeding His profound call on her life to begin writing biblical journals. As she started her new life, her eyes were opened to the supernatural miracles that God was creating around her, and Training Your Children to Remain in the Vine shares what she and her family has learned from experiencing God's blessings and miracles. Terita and her husband, Nolan (aka Saint), are thankful for the gift of salvation and for the ability to love God, to love others, and to help others get to know Christ on a deeper level.

Printed in the United States
by Baker & Taylor Publisher Services